The Holly ana tne Ivy

A Play in Three Acts

by Wynyard Browne

SERVING THEATRE

SINCE 1830

WWW.SAMUELFRENCH.CO.UK
WWW.SAMUELFRENCH.COM

The Holly and the Ivy

By arrangement with Frith Banbury Ltd.

TENNENT PRODUCTIONS LTD.

(in association with the Arts Council of Great Britain)

first presented this play at the Lyric Theatre, Hammersmith, in March 1950 with the following cast

The Rev. MARTIN GREGORY	*Herbert Lomas*
JENNY, his elder daughter	*Jane Baxter*
MARGARET, his younger daughter..	*Daphne Arthur*
MICK, his son	*Bryan Forbes*
AUNT LYDIA, his sister-in-law	*Margaret Halstan*
AUNT BRIDGET, his sister	*Maureen Delany*
RICHARD WYNDHAM, cousin of his late wife ..	*Patrick Waddington*
DAVID PATERSON	*Andrew Crawford*

and subsequently at the Duchess Theatre, London

Directed by FRITH BANBURY

Setting by TANYA MOISEIWITSCH

The play takes place in the living room of a vicarage in Norfolk.

SCENES

ACT I
Christmas Eve.

ACT II
After dinner, the same evening. (The lights are lowered
to denote the passage of two hours.)

ACT III
Christmas morning.

No reference is intended in this play to any person, alive or dead.

AUTHOR'S NOTE TO PRODUCERS

" THE HOLLY AND THE IVY " is, above all, a play of mood. It was suggested by the sight of a snow-covered tree outside a window on a lowering December afternoon and by the thought of those faded, melancholy Georgian vicarages, scattered all over Norfolk, in every village and country town, centres of a decaying Christian tradition, where the cross-currents of family feeling have an especial poignancy at Christmas time.

" The holly bears a savour as bitter as any gall " says the carol, and these words might describe the sudden pang which most people have felt at some period of their lives during the festivities of Christmas, a cold breath of the irony which lurks at the heart of a great festival of religious rejoicing in a sceptical age.

It is this irony of Christmas which disturbs and blows away the mists of habit, so that the characters, during the course of the play, come to see each other for the first time as they really are; and the reality seems to them at first as strange and new as the familiar Norfolk landscape outside their windows, after a night when snow has fallen.

This is the sort of note to be struck in the production of the play—rather than the note of jolly, cosy family comedy—or the brisker, intellectual note of a debate about whether or not you can tell the truth to a parson.

Almost every scene in the play is capable of misproduction in either of these two ways—the scene in Act 1 (where Mick and David put up the holly) which should be desultory, meditative, almost poetic, as well as comic, can very easily deteriorate into a trivial, purely domestic comedy scene where all the fun depends simply on the idea of two males putting up holly. This tends to strike audiences as irresistibly funny in itself, unless very carefully rehearsed and timed in order not to shatter the mood.

The big scene between Margaret and her father in Act 3 *can* seem like a rather elementary theological debate instead of what is intended—the gradual revelation to Margaret, taking place before the eyes of the audience, of the true nature of her father. To achieve this it is *essential* that Gregory should seem to be thinking and talking as much of himself as of her, and that she should really be aware of the personality he is thus revealing to her.

Similarly, the pathos underlying the comedy must never be lost. Gregory talking about the Incas in Act 1—and about the origins of Christmas customs in Act 2—is *not* the comedy of a garrulous old man but a revelation of the fact that this obscure old parson is a man of culture and wide-ranging imagination, absent-minded only because the whole of world history is in his mind.

Jenny must not seem merely " the domestic type ", but someone of very special qualities enslaved by domestic duties. " It's odd how people get thought of simply as what they do " she says to David; and every moment, however small, when she has a chance to think of something other than tea-trays, whether it be wild duck in China or the white owl in the garden, should be given its full value—but without a trace of self consciousness.

Aunt Lydia must not be just silly and gushing, but " strange and grand " as Jenny says. She has a real, not an assumed, Grand Duchess quality. She has the imagination and has actually experienced a great love. Let the actress play the part seriously and it will be funny. Let her try to be funny and it will seem stagey, gushing, and a bore.

Aunt Bridget is, of course, the boldest comedy figure but she too has pathos. Her coming downstairs " with these few trifles " in the last Act can and should be very moving if properly played. Her curt explosiveness is an Irish way of covering great sensibility and a fear of being snubbed.

Some critics described Gregory as an old man who has to be " wrapped in cotton-wool " by his family. This is a misunderstanding. The difficulty which all the children, but especially Margaret and Mick, have in talking freely before him, comes more from an uneasy desire to protect themselves from the force of a stronger personality than from a simple desire to protect him. They are afraid of the magnitude of the conflict which will be produced between two attitudes of life, theirs and his. It is worth remembering that Gregory is not, but only thinks himself, a failure.

Throughout the play the pauses, the changes of tempo, the changes of mood, not only between scene and scene but within the characters themselves as they speak, are of the utmost importance—perhaps especially in the somnolent close of the evening in the second half of Act 2 which, if carefully played as a pattern of mood, has a drama of its own, quite apart from being an effective preparation for what is going to happen.

Rightly produced, the keynote of the whole play could seem to be sounded in the first half of Act 2 by Jenny's remark, dropped as it were from far away into the uneasy silence which succeeds Richard's tactful drinking up of the whisky which Margaret has violently refused—" How bitter the holly smells. . . ."—a line which, like many of the best moments in the play, was invented by my wife, who did so much work on the play that I am often ashamed not to have called it a collaboration.

WYNYARD BROWNE

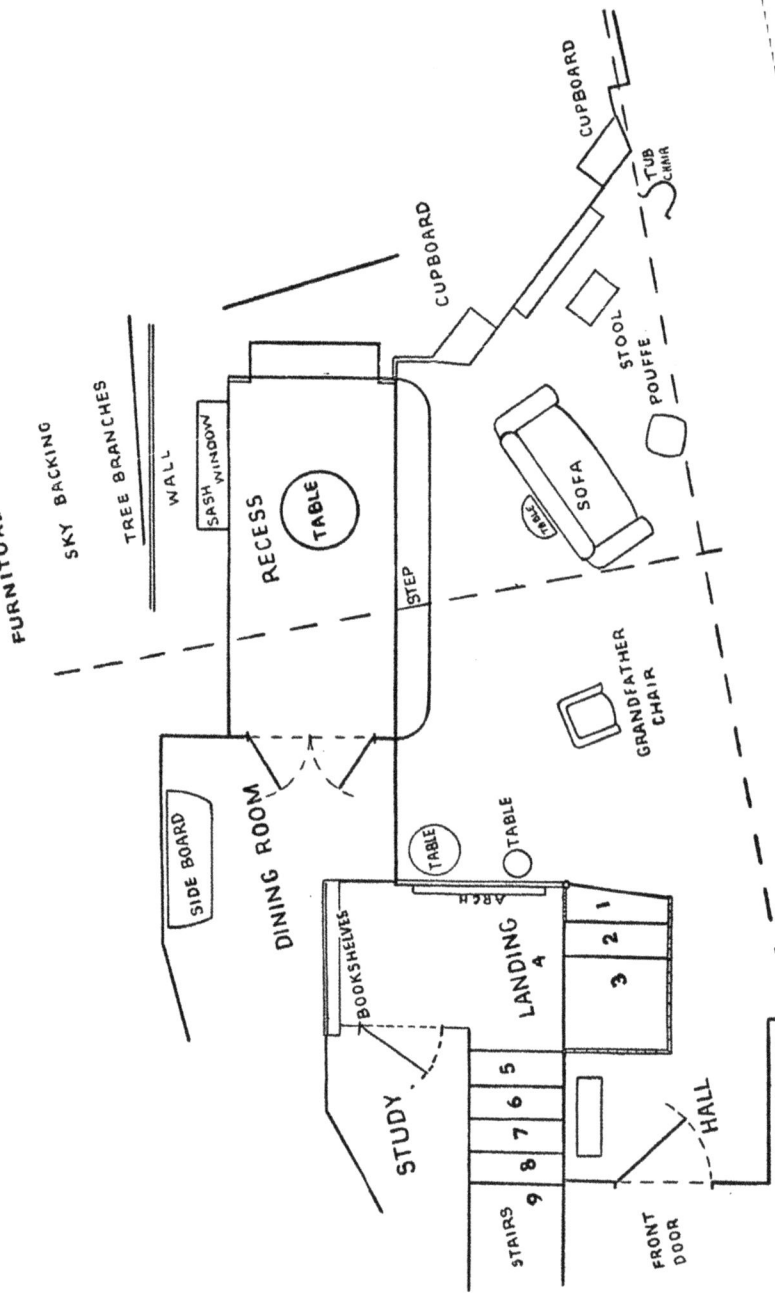
FURNITURE AS SET FOR ACT II

SKY BACKING

TREE BRANCHES

WALL

SASH WINDOW

RECESS

TABLE

CUPBOARD

CUPBOARD

STOOL

POUFFE

TUB CHAIR

SOFA

TABLE

STEP

GRANDFATHER CHAIR

SIDE BOARD

DINING ROOM

BOOKSHELVES

TABLE

TABLE

ARCH

STUDY

LANDING

STAIRS

HALL

FRONT DOOR

THE HOLLY AND THE IVY

ACT I

The whole play takes place in the living-room of a Georgian vicarage in Norfolk. The room is pleasant but faded, even shabby here and there—and a little melancholy.

[The most prominent feature is a large, sash window at back, with white-painted shutters and seat. Through it can be seen part of a tree, black against the lowering sky of a December afternoon in Act I, snow-covered and sunlit against blue sky in Act III; in Act II, the shutters are closed.

On actor's R., *first the hall with the front door up and down stage and almost out of sight, then two steps up (up and down stage) to a landing with banisters. From the landing stairs go up towards* R. *to the bedrooms. Upstage of the stairs—the study door. Upstage of the two steps on to the landing an arch with banisters.*

From this the back wall runs plain for some four feet and is completed by a recess raised one step up; R. *of the recess, double doors to the dining-room run up and down stage. The* L. *corner of the recess is formed by two deeply recessed and shuttered windows— one in the back wall, one up and down stage.*

The L. *wall rakes on considerably and comprises the chimney breast and fireplace with table-height cupboards up and down stage of it with shallow, arched recesses above them.*

The hall has heavy curtains across the opening; they are drawn across throughout Act II, and the hallstand is above the door on and off stage. Above the two steps and below the banisters, a small, pedestal wine table. R.C., *some four feet on stage from the two steps, a Victorian grandfather chair. In the* R. *corner, on a round table, the Christmas tree, decorated with tinsel, coloured balls and candles. Downstage of the double doors, but on the rostrum of the recess, a small, oblong table to be used for a lamp and the drinks. On* the back wall of the recess a grandfather clock and two Victorian occasional chairs. C. of the recess a round, pedestal table for the honesty and presents. The windows have pelmets and heavy curtains. At right angles to the fireplace, with room to pass between it and the fireplace flat, a large chesterfield (described throughout as " sofa ") with loose, chintz cover. In front of the fire a stool, chair height. In front of the sofa, a low pouffe. Below the fire and facing on and up stage, a Victorian tub chair. Behind the sofa a half circular table (described throughout as " sofa table ").

Light fittings comprise a hanging lamp in the hall, a bracket and switch below it at the foot of the stairs. A table lamp on the table by double doors. A pair of brackets either side of the grandfather clock on the back wall of the recess. A standard lamp between the L. window and the cupboard above the fire. A pair of brackets on the chimney breast. A table lamp on the cupboard below the fire and a chandelier centre of the ceiling. There are three switches by the double doors. A small wireless set stands on the cupboard upstage of the fire.

For the opening of Act I, the furniture has been disarranged to enable JENNY to do the decorating. A step-ladder is below the chandelier. Downstage of it a dust sheet on the floor with a pile of holly and ivy. Down R.C., an occasional chair with its back to the audience and a box of decorations on it. The grandfather chair is pushed against the wall up R., between the Christmas tree and the double doors with its back onstage. The half circular sofa table is in the recess under the L. window. The sofa is pushed back up and down stage with its back to the fire and nearly up to the recess, but there is room to pass between it and the fireplace flat. The fire-stool and the pouffe have been put on it to be out of the way. A paper chain hangs from the up R. corner to the chandelier. Another from the up L. corner has not yet been secured to the chandelier and is draped over the standard lamp. Holly and ivy decorate the pictures, light fittings and banisters, except those places to be done during the action. Christmas cards decorate the mantelpiece and cupboards above and below the fire.]

Christmas Eve. A lowering December afternoon, heavy with snow.

JENNY *is on a step-ladder, fixing paper decorations to the chandelier,* C. *The carol service from King's is on the wireless. They are singing: " O come, O come, Emmanuel ". A young man in a raincoat enters through the hall opening and makes a noise to attract her attention.*

DAVID (*coming to* R. *of her step-ladder*). Whit! Hey, Jenny!

JENNY (*startled*). David!

DAVID (*has a wry Scotch manner and the forceful yet musical accent peculiar to Aberdeenshire*). Anyone arrived yet?

JENNY. No, but they soon will. What time is it?

DAVID. Half-past three. Quarter to four maybe. (*Removing his coat and hanging it in hall.*)

JENNY. Is that all? How dark it is.

DAVID. Ay, it's a murky afternoon. I'm thinkin' there's snow coming. Will I turn that thing off? (*Indicating wireless set which is above fireplace* L.)

JENNY. Don't you like carols?

DAVID. Ay, they're all right. But I want some talk with you before they all come.

JENNY. There's no more to be said. I wonder if I've put too much ivy. . . . (*Looks round the room.*)

DAVID. There's a lot more to be said, if you ask me. Will I turn this off?

JENNY. Wait a moment. Listen, it's so lovely. (*They both listen in silence till the carol finishes.*) It's odd how sound can be so beautifully still.

DAVID. Ay, it's beautiful. Will I turn it off all the same? (*Crossing below step-ladder and sofa to do so.*)

JENNY (*laughing*). If you must. Just pass me that chain over there, will you?

DAVID (*bringing her the end of chain which was draped on standard lamp above fireplace and to* L. *of her*). What on earth are you doing all this for? Have you got children coming or what?

JENNY (*attaching chain to chandelier*). No, no children. Just ourselves and the people we always have for Christmas. You know, that cousin of my mother's, Richard Wyndham, and a couple of elderly aunts.

DAVID. What would your elderly aunts be wanting with all this?

JENNY. It's only what we always do. I don't want this Christmas to fall flat just because mother's not here. Don't you like it?

DAVID. Ay, it's pretty. But it's an awfu' waste of time.

JENNY. Oh, no. It isn't, David. It's part of something very important—the very thing that *is* Christmas for most people —that feeling in the air, the feeling that everything's different . . . special . . . pass me that star, will you?

DAVID. I think ye're mad. Stark, staring, raving mad. Come down off that ladder. (*Down stage of step-ladder.*)

JENNY. No, David. I must finish. They'll be here soon.

DAVID (*to R. of step-ladder*). Come on down. I want to talk to you. (*He seizes her round the waist, lifts her down and kisses her. She is obviously very much in love with him. After a moment still holding her, he says softly.*) Darling.

JENNY (*echoes him*). Darling. (*Then her mood changes suddenly; she sighs; flatly, her head on his shoulder.*) I suppose those people who fall asleep in the snow feel like this. They know they've got to keep awake at all costs; but they can't help giving up the struggle just for a moment, because the snow's so warm and cosy.

DAVID. I never heard of anyone yet freezin' to death from a kiss.

JENNY (*laughing and moving away slightly to L.C.*). No, but . . . well, it's all so pointless, isn't it? It gets us nowhere.

DAVID (*following to R. of her*). I don't know about that. It's got a lot of people quite a long way before now. (*Tries to kiss her again.*)

JENNY (*avoids him and moves away below step-ladder to mantelpiece*). No, David, please. (*Starts arranging Christmas cards*

on mantelpiece, making conversation.) You haven't met Aunt
Lydia, have you?

DAVID *(following her to R.C.).* Is that the old Irish termagant
you had the sharp post card from yesterday?

JENNY *(laughing).* No, that's Aunt Bridget. *(She switches on
standard lamp above fire.)* She's a Gregory. Aunt Lydia's
mummy's sister. She's quite different. She's rather grand
and strange. She's the widow of a King's Messenger.
(Arranging Christmas cards on mantelpiece.)

DAVID. Jenny . . .

JENNY *(continuing firmly).* He died when they'd only been
married a year or two; but ever since, she's gone about
feeling she has a special understanding of men.

DAVID *(cutting across all this).* Jenny, I've heard. *(She stiffens.)*
It's all fixed. *(Coming behind her.)* They want me to sail
at the end of January. That's what I came to tell you.
They've written to know will I be taking my wife with me.
I told them " yes ".

JENNY *(turning to face him).* Oh, David, why? You know it's
impossible.

DAVID. It's not impossible at all.

JENNY. Yes, it is. Quite impossible. You know I can't leave
Father.

DAVID. That's absurd. Of course you can.

JENNY. Darling, it's not absurd. There's no one else; I must
look after him Can't you understand . . . *(She hesitates.)*
I *must.*

DAVID. That's all nonsense. *(Moving away to C.)* Children
can't be expected to sacrifice their lives to their parents like
that. It's not within reason. When it comes to a conflict
between the young and the old, it's the old that have to give
way. That's the nature of things. Otherwise, human life
couldn't go on. *(Returning to her.)* Each generation'd be a
dead end.

JENNY. You're talking like a text-book, David.

DAVID. Maybe I am, but. . . . Oh, Jenny, you know me. I haven't the words of my own for saying these things. But you know what I mean. . . . Look here, what there is between you and me is . . . central to the world. It's . . . what the whole of life depends on. It's much too important to be sacrificed to the interests of the old. That's why there's always a conflict.

JENNY. But this isn't " a conflict between the young and the old ". It's what I feel for someone I love.

DAVID (*teasing her*). Don't you love me, too? (JENNY *just looks at him.*) Well, then. It's suicidal. Ye're twenty-nine now. I won't be back from South America for five years. You'll be thirty-four then. That's middle-age.

JENNY. I know. (*Turning away.*)

DAVID (*seeing the look on her face and putting his hand on her shoulder*). Oh, Jenny, don't. . . . I shouldn't have said that. It's not true anyway. Thirty-four's nothing. I'm thirty-four myself; there's nothing to worry about, Jenny. I'll have a word with your father.

JENNY. No! No, David, you mustn't.

DAVID. Why not? He's a reasonable man. He wouldn't expect you. . . .

JENNY. Of course he wouldn't. (*Crossing him to box of decorations on chair down* R.C.) Oh, you don't understand! That's the whole point. If Daddy knew about us, he'd never ask me to stay, however much he wanted me. He wouldn't *let* me stay. But that wouldn't make it any easier for me to go, would it? When I know that he needs me. Don't you see? That's why he mustn't know about you and me at all, it would worry him dreadfully. You won't tell him, will you? Promise?

DAVID. I'm not making any promises.

(MR. GREGORY *comes in hastily from the study, just woken from sleep. He is a large, elderly clergyman. Though he has lived most of his life in England, he still speaks with*

*an Irish accent. He is mild, scholarly and a little vague, but
not in the least eccentric.*)

GREGORY. Ach, good gracious, I've been asleep. What time
is it?

JENNY. Quarter to four.

GREGORY. Is that all? Are ye sure? Hullo, David. (*At
bottom step.*)

DAVID. Good afternoon.

(GREGORY *suddenly becomes giddy, closes his eyes and
stands for a moment leaning against the wall for support.*)

JENNY (*going to* L. *of him*). What's the matter? Are you
all right?

GREGORY. Yes, yes, I'm all right. (*Crossing* JENNY *to* C.) A
bit giddy for a moment, that's all. It's nothing. I woke
with a start, ye see, thinkin' I'd forgotten all about the
children. It's so dark in there this afternoon I thought it
was much later.

JENNY. What children?

GREGORY. I've got to go down to the schools. The infants
are having their Christmas treat.

JENNY. *You* needn't go surely?

GREGORY. I must. I promised Miss Coleman I'd look in.

JENNY. But you've a heavy day to-morrow; and you're not
well.

GREGORY (*impatiently*). If I'm not well enough to do me work,
I'd better give up, that's all. (*There is a slight embarrassed
pause.*) How about you, David? Have you heard anything
yet?

DAVID. Ay, it's all fixed. I was just telling Jenny. I'm to sail
at the end of January. (JENNY *goes into hall for* GREGORY'S
overcoat.)

GREGORY. Ah, you're a lucky fellow. D'ye know I've always
wanted to go to South America ever since I was a boy?
When I was first ordained, I made up me mind to go out

there—as a missionary, you know. But it never came off
. . . I never meant to stay pottering about here in England
all me life . . . (JENNY *returns with his coat to down* R.) Ah
well, there it is . . . But South America's always had a
fascination for me, ever since I first read Prescott—" The
Conquest of Peru "—that's a wonderful book now. Have
ye ever read it?

DAVID. I can't say that I have.

GREGORY. It's about the place somewhere. D'ye know where
it is, Jenny? A great fat red book with gold toolin' on it.
I won it as a praemium for Latin verses when I was at school
in Dublin. That was the first time I ever realized the size
of human history—all that part about the Incas. Remarkable people, the Incas. Great mathematicians, you know,
and sun-worshippers.

DAVID (*blankly*). Is that so?

GREGORY (*sweeping on enthusiastically*). D'ye know the most
interesting thing? They were the first people in the world
to discover about manure. (JENNY *laughs*.) No, but it's
true. You better tell your father about that. He'd be
interested, being a farmer. They were the first people to
discover the value of guano as a fertilizer. It's the deposit
of the sea-birds, you know; it's found all down the Western
Coasts. Now it's a great modern industry, the import and
export of guano . . . all discovered by the old Incas. They
were a great, civilized people and now there's scarcely a
trace of them left . . .

DAVID. I don't expect I'll be having much to do with all that:
I'm going out there to build airports.

GREGORY. Airports . . . Ah, well, people seem to want
airports, I can't think why, but they do. D'ye know, I
often think it'd be very pleasant to be an engineer or something like that—to be doin' something that people want.
That's the worst of being a parson. People don't want you.
At least, they do and they don't. If you *don't* go and visit

them they say " It's disgraceful. Here have I been living in the place six months and the parson never near me ". And if you do go, they say, " Ach, look who's here. What's he want to come pokin' and pryin' for? Stickin' his nose in where he's not wanted ".

JENNY. Hadn't you better go, darling, if you are going?

GREGORY. What? (*Going to* JENNY R.) Oh, good Lord, yes. The treat. I forgot.

JENNY. Here's your coat then. (*Helps him into it.*) You'd better have your scarf too. It's bitterly cold. And you'll need a torch for coming back. (*Goes to fetch them from hall.*)

GREGORY. Her mother was just the same, you know, David. I don't know where I'd be without her.

JENNY (*coming back, giving him scarf, hat and torch*). There. Are you sure you're all right now? Hadn't you better have a little whisky before you go?

GREGORY. Whisky, that reminds me. Have we whisky in the house for Richard?

JENNY (*goes below* DAVID *and up to cupboard above fireplace*). I think there ought to be enough here. I'll just see. (*Takes out bottle.*) It's nearly full.

GREGORY. D'ye think one bottle's enough for him?

JENNY. Well, surely! He'll only be here for two or three days. Nobody else'll drink it.

GREGORY. All right then. Leave it out on the side where he can help himself.

JENNY. But he'll drink it all. Doctor Morris says we must always have some in the house for you.

GREGORY. Ach, nonsense! I don't want the stuff. Leave it on the side.

JENNY. But it's so frightfully expensive. We can't have Richard helping himself whenever he likes.

GREGORY. We can't ask people here then, if we can't afford to entertain them properly. (JENNY *goes above sofa and puts*

B

whisky bottle on table below dining-room doors.) What about you, David? Would you care to take a glass?

DAVID. No, thanks.

JENNY (*coming down* R. *of* GREGORY). Darling, you *must* go. You don't want to be out when they all arrive.

GREGORY. When is Margaret coming?

JENNY. I've arranged with Richard to call for her after lunch and drive her down. I made him promise to get her here in time for tea.

GREGORY. You haven't met me younger daughter, have you, David? (DAVID *is still* L.C.) Of course we don't see her very often now. She's a journalist, you know. She writes these articles on fashions for the ladies' magazines. You wouldn't think that'd be an interesting subject now, would you? You know it's an extraordinary thing, but I find meself getting enthralled reading about the autumn collections and . . . what's this it was I was reading out about at lunch, Jenny?

JENNY. " The season's silhouette "?

GREGORY. That's it. " The season's silhouette." D'ye know the trouble they take with the silhouette now? I'd no idea of it. Hip-lines, waist-lines and—what's this they call them? Foundation-garments.

DAVID. Ay, it's almost a branch of engineering.

GREGORY. D'ye know what they've taken to wearing now? The latest line is . . . (*He can't find the word for it.*) Ach, there's an article here somewhere Margaret was writin' about it . . . (*Starting to move upstage between step-ladder and sofa as if to get magazine from cupboard above fireplace.*)

JENNY. Daddy darling, you must go.

GREGORY. Yes, yes, Jenny. (*He stops and crosses below her to hall.*) I'm off. This minute. This minute. I'll show you some other time, David. (*He goes.*)

JENNY. You see, David. (*Turns to him and then picks up star from box on chair down* R.C. *and goes up step-ladder to fix it.*)

DAVID. Ay. (*Pause.*) What about this sister of yours? Why can't she come home? (*To foot of step-ladder.*)

JENNY. Margaret? She won't come.

DAVID. Why not?

JENNY. She just won't. She's got her job and her friends in London. She wouldn't come and bury herself here in the country. No. The obvious person is Daddy's sister, Aunt Bridget. But Daddy and she don't get on. They never have. And she's got that explosive Irish temper that goes off like a squib at the slightest touch.

DAVID. What about your other aunt, the one that understands men?

JENNY (*laughing and coming down off step-ladder*). Wait till you see her. She's a hopeless neurotic. She's lived all her life in hotels and she can't even make a piece of toast. Anyway, she's nearly eighty. (*Pause.*) Over there, please David. (DAVID *takes step-ladder to fireplace and puts it with steps upstage.*) It's no use. I'm the only one. I've got to stay. (JENNY *goes to box of decorations* R.C.)

DAVID. I don't accept that. You could find him a housekeeper, couldn't you? As long as there's someone competent in the house, it's not such a terrible thing for a man to live alone, is it?

JENNY. Yes, David, it is. At least it would be for him. (*Crossing to step-ladder with* DAVID *upstage of her.*) It'd be far worse for him than for an ordinary person.

DAVID. I don't see why.

JENNY (*going up step-ladder to decorate lamp bracket with ivy*). It's always worse for a parson anyway. He can't do the most ordinary things, simply because he is a parson. For instance, he can't just drop into the pub for company when he's bored in the evenings. People don't want him.

DAVID. Of course not. A pub's no place for a parson.

JENNY. No, but it's the same wherever he goes, whatever he does; people don't feel free to behave naturally when he's there.

DAVID (*sitting on downstage arm of sofa*). Ay, I know what you mean. There's an awkwardness. I've noticed it meself in railway carriages. Everyone stops talking for a moment when a parson gets in; and when they do start again, things aren't quite the same. They became unnatural with each other, too.

JENNY. That's just it. A parson's set apart, isolated. But it's not only that. You know Daddy. He's essentially bookish, scholarly. (*Sitting on step-ladder.*) Look at the way he was talking to you about the Incas just now. He was brilliant as a young man, and all his friends were the kind of people who have since become dons, K.C.s, and high-up civil servants who sit on Royal Commissions. But he's quite lost touch with them. Now they're only names he reads in the newspapers. Because he chose to be a parson, he's become separated from people with his own interests, his own outlook; and he's had to spend half his life organizing bazaars and going to Sunday school treats, doing silly trivial things with silly trivial people—oh, well, that's not fair, I suppose they're just ordinary people. But to me it seems such a *waste*. He gets on with them well enough and they like him. But they don't understand him and they've nothing in common with him. I think that's largely why we, the family, have always meant so much to him. (*Standing up to resume decorating.*)

DAVID. Couldn't he get a job somewhere else? In a big town where there'd be more chance of intellectual companionship?

JENNY. He's too old to start all over again in a new parish. He ought to retire really. But he's got to hold on for another five years, till he gets a pension.

DAVID. Ay, it's a difficult situation, I see that. But I don't see why it should fall on you. (*Rising to face her.*) That sister of yours must take her turn.

JENNY. I've told you. She won't.

DAVID. That's absurd. She's bloody well got to. What on earth's the matter with her?

JENNY. Oh, she's all right really. (*Coming down step-ladder.*) I'm very fond of her. But . . . well, she's different. I suppose, being older, I've always felt more responsible.

DAVID. Ay, and you'd feel that more, being the home-making type.

JENNY (*pause; she looks at him for a moment*). You don't really know me, do you? It's odd how people get thought of simply as what they do, whether they've chosen to do it or not. . . . When we were small I was always the one who wanted to get away from home. . . . Margaret was the stay-at-home. She didn't even want to go to school. She loved being at home. She loved everything to do with it. I've always wanted to be more a part of what's going on in the world. But somehow it hasn't turned out like that. Whatever happened *I* never got away, because of mother being ill. Margaret's work took her away all the time, Rome, Stockholm, America, London . . . I don't really think she enjoys it, either.

DAVID. Well then, if she likes being at home . . .?

JENNY. She doesn't any longer. She seems quite changed.

DAVID. Does she know about you and me?

JENNY. You always seem to forget, David. No one knows. (*Crossing to box of decorations on chair* R.C.)

DAVID (*following to* L. *of her*). But, if you told her, surely she'd help you out a bit? After all, she's had her chance. She's been knockin' about London all these years. She's had plenty of opportunity to pick up a man. You've managed *that* for yourself anyway, even if you have been stuck away in the country. That gives you a sort of biological priority. Even in the eyes of the Government. Any woman'd recognize that, let alone your own sister. I'm sure, if you asked her, she'd give you a break.

JENNY. It's a lot to ask, you know, David. I'm afraid it's not as simple as that.

DAVID. Well, *will* you ask her, anyway?

JENNY. I'll ask her, yes; but I'm pretty sure it won't be any use. You may as well make up your mind to that.

DAVID. Ye're not going to let everything depend on *her* surely?

JENNY. It does, I'm afraid. It just does.

DAVID (*going up* C.). But that's preposterous! You can't just sit down and let the whole future of two people depend on what someone else chooses to do. It's monstrous! (*Coming back to* L. *of her.*)

JENNY. But . . . doesn't everyone always depend on what other people choose to do? Isn't that why it's so very important what we choose?

DAVID. Ay, it's important all right. It's important to you and me now. (*Pause;* JENNY *doesn't answer;* DAVID *walks away towards* L.C.; *says very quietly, not looking at her.*) This is the sort of job I've had in mind ever since I started to qualify. For nearly twenty years, ever since I was fourteen, I've been working towards a job like this. But if I have to choose between it and you, it's no use to me.

JENNY (*who has not looked at him and is thinking of her father*). The really important thing is never to choose to do what destroys other people. Isn't that—well, isn't it the whole meaning of being good?

DAVID. Being good? You're *too* good. That's your trouble. If you're not careful, you'll be destroying yourself—and me too. You're so good that it becomes bad. (JENNY *weeps;* DAVID *comes to her.*) Jenny, Jenny, don't. I don't mean to upset you. (*Putting his arms round her.*) What's the matter, Jenny? Tell me.

JENNY. Only . . . only what you said . . . that goodness can destroy people.

DAVID. That's all nonsense. Never heed what I say.

JENNY. But is it true, David? Can it be true?

DAVID. Don't ask me. I'm only an engineer.

MICK (*offstage*). Anybody there?

JENNY. Mick!

(JENNY's *younger brother*, MICHAEL, *who is of call-up age, bursts into the room.* DAVID *steps back so that* MICK *comes to between them.*)

MICK. Hullo, chums.

JENNY. Mick! How did you get here? (*They kiss each other.*)

MICK. Hitch-hiked—Hullo David.

JENNY. I thought you weren't coming. You said you couldn't get leave.

MICK. I wangled it. Forty-eight hours. Compassionate.

JENNY. Compassionate?

MICK. The army's very sentimental at Christmas. The great, ruthless machine suddenly goes soft in the middle, like bad fruit. It's rather sinister.

JENNY. What *are* you talking about?

DAVID. How did you fix it?

MICK. Went to see the Major—and pitched a tale. That's one small advantage of being Irish. I told him my mother had recently died, my father's getting old and my little sister—oh, you ought to know my little sister, she's wonderful—is bravely struggling to keep things going. She wants us all home for Christmas this year, because maybe it's the last Christmas we'll all spend together in the old home. It worked like magic. I'd almost swear when I'd finished there were tears in the Major's eyes. " England won't go far wrong, Gregory, as long as men feel like you do about their homes."

JENNY. Mick, you're awful. How could you?

MICK. Why? What's wrong? It's all true, isn't it?

JENNY. No, it's not. Not a word of it's true. You don't feel like that at all. (MICK *looks disconcerted.*) I'm sorry. I suppose I'm being silly. I expect it's all right, really. Look, could you and David finish putting up the holly for me? I must go and get tea ready. They'll all be here soon. (*She goes up between* MICK *and* DAVID *and out through dining-room.*)

MICK. What's the matter with her?

DAVID. She's worried about your father, I think. He wasn't very well just now. (*Going to get holly from pile on dust-sheet* C.)

MICK. O Lord. He never seems to be well these days. What about this damned holly?

DAVID. You do that side of the room, I'll do this.

MICK (*going into hall to take off great-coat*). Right. Just stick it behind the pictures. Anywhere you can get it to stay. (*Returning to* R. *of dust-sheet to get holly.*)

DAVID. You know, it's a strange thing but I find all this Christmas decoration peculiarly depressing. (*Having select. d holly goes up step-ladder to decorate the picture above fireplace.*)

MICK (*preoccupied with holly*). M'm. It is a bit depressing.

DAVID. As a matter of fact, any form of public rejoicing always afflicts me with melancholia. I'm always thankful I escaped being in London on V.E. day. That must've been terrible. Ten million people all rejoicing in the streets. I'd have been suicidal. That's the trouble with me. I'm an individualist.

MICK. M'm. I expect that's the trouble with me, too. I can't bear Christmas. I used to like it as a child; but now . . . it's . . . well, as you say, it's depressing. (*Stands on grandfather chair up* R. *to put holly on pictures on wall above it.*) We've got a dozen aunts coming.

DAVID. I thought it was two.

MICK. There you are, you see—accurate. Sound, reliable, accurate. I wish to God I was like that. (*The piece of holly he has been arranging pricks him.*) Damn! (*Starts again—pause—*) What's the matter with my father, do you know?

DAVID. He was a bit giddy for a moment, that's all. (*Coming down step-ladder to get more holly from pile* C.)

MICK. He ought to retire, you know.

DAVID. I gather he can't afford to.

MICK. It's not that. He could; but he won't. *I'm* the trouble really.

DAVID. Why you?

MICK. He wants me to go to Cambridge. That costs money. I'm not the type to get scholarships. Anyway, I've got a year to do in the army first. That means at least four more years for him in this place. I don't want him to kill himself for me. Anyway, it's not worth it. (*Getting off chair and coming down for holly*.) I don't even know that I want to go to Cambridge.

DAVID (*returning to and going up ladder with more holly*). There's a lot of advantages to be had from a university education, you know.

MICK. By me? I'm not the type. No good telling him that, though. He always says the years he was up at Cambridge were the best and most valuable three years of his life; and he wants me to have them too. It wouldn't be so bad if I knew what I wanted to do. But I don't. I just want to live. What *is* it that makes people want to do one particular thing in life rather than anything else? I don't seem to be made that way. That's the trouble with me. No bent. (*Getting up on to grandfather chair again with holly*.) Were you *born* wanting to be an engineer?

DAVID. I can't exactly remember. As a small boy I was always tinkering.

MICK (*after pause, while they concentrate on putting up the holly*). Do you suppose people are born wanting to be clergymen?

DAVID. I should hardly think it very likely.

MICK. That's something that's always interested me. What happens to *them*? What makes a chap, at the age of eighteen or twenty, suddenly decide to become a *parson*? God knows there's not much—what do they call it?—incentive. It's a hell of a life. What makes them do it?

DAVID (*coming down off ladder and backing away down c. to admire his work*). Maybe they have some kind of mystical experience—a sudden flash of insight into the meaning of life. (*Pointing to holly*.) How does this look?

MICK. Looks all right to me. How about mine?

DAVID. It's a wee bit lop-sided. (*Goes to pick up more holly from pile.*)

MICK. There you are, you see. I'm no good. I can't even do this. (*Pause; he re-arranges holly.*) Have you ever had one?

DAVID. One what?

MICK. A mystical experience—what was it you said?—a sudden flash of insight into the meaning of life?

DAVID. I can't say I have.

MICK. Nor me. (*Sitting on back of grandfather chair, his feet on the seat.*) What do you make of it all? Religion and so forth? Do you believe in God?

DAVID. What's the matter with you this afternoon?

MICK. Oh, I don't know . . . Christmas . . . coming home . . . (*Coming down to R. of pile of holly.*) You probably can't realize what it's like to grow up in the atmosphere of a vicarage.

DAVID. I can't see much wrong with this atmosphere. (*Going up step-ladder again.*)

MICK. No, but however pleasant and easy they are, always there's a subtle pressure on you all the time to think and feel things you don't naturally think and feel. And you see what that leads to? If you're not careful, you get involved in a kind of perpetual pretence. It's a difficult business having a parson for a father.

DAVID. Jenny seems to do all right.

MICK. Oh, Jenny, yes . . . Margaret doesn't.

DAVID. Is that why she doesn't come home much these days?

MICK. Well, that's my guess. Can't think of any other reason. Let's have a little more light on the scene. (*Going up to table lamp on table below dining-room doors.*) Gosh, look at that sky. It's heavy with snow. (*Switches on lamp.*) When you come to think of it, Jenny's rather a special person, you know. Of course, Margaret's remarkable, but Jenny's . . .

DAVID. I know what you mean. Jenny's got a kind of natural magic.

(*Front door bell rings.* DAVID *comes down from ladder.*)

MICK. Oh, lord, that'll be the Aunts.

(JENNY *comes in from dining-room, puts down tray with glasses and water on table by dining-room doors, switches on bracket and chandelier lights by dining-room door.*)

DAVID (*quickly*). I think I'll be getting along now. We've a gathering of the clans too.

JENNY. Oh, no. Don't go. I want you to meet Margaret. Mick go and let them in, will you? Oh, wait a minute. Just get rid of that holly first. Put it in the hall.

(MICK *begins to gather up holly on dust-sheet.*)

DAVID. What about the step-ladder?

JENNY. Oh, yes, could you put it away? You know where it goes. (*She goes up to windows, closes shutters and draws curtains;* DAVID *takes steps off to dining-room.*)

MICK (*pricking himself and dropping sheet*). Damn!

(*Bell rings peremptorily.*)

All right. All right. (*Picks up sheet with holly, runs with it to hall. There is nowhere to put it there, so throws it in grandfather chair and runs to let them in, switching on hall light as he goes.*)

(*Voices in the hall.*)

BRIDGET. Had you forgotten we were coming or what? Me feet are freezin' to the doorstep.

LYDIA. Siberia, it's like Siberia. Dear Mick, how nice to see you. I didn't think you'd be here.

MICK. Wait a moment. I'll take those.

BRIDGET. What are ye doin' hangin' about here? I thought you'd be overseas by now.

LYDIA. How nice you look in your uniform. Don't you think it suits him, Bridget?

28 THE HOLLY AND THE IVY [ACT I

(DAVID *enters from dining-room to up* L.C.)

BRIDGET. I prefer the naval uniform myself. (*To* MICK.) Be careful of that one, there's breakables in it.

(*The* AUNTS, LYDIA *and* BRIDGET *come in.* LYDIA, *tall and rather grand, has a sweeping, emotional manner.* BRIDGET, *who is obviously much poorer, is explosive and has a strong Irish accent.* LYDIA *comes first to* R. *of* JENNY *who is* R.C. BRIDGET *follows to behind* LYDIA.)

LYDIA. What a journey! We're frozen. Jenny darling, how are you? (*Kisses and embraces her.*) We've been travelling across Russia—miles and miles of frozen fen . . . and government pine forests . . . and the heating in the carriage seemed to have jammed—it's exactly how I imagine Russia to be. (JENNY *tries to escape.*) Wait, let me have a look at you. . . . You're tired, my darling, you've been doing too much.

JENNY. Hullo, Aunt Bridget. How are you? (*Crossing* LYDIA *to greet* BRIDGET.)

BRIDGET (*coldly*). I'm all right, thanks. (*Nods towards* DAVID.) Who's this?

JENNY. Oh, I'm sorry. This is a friend of ours, David Paterson.

LYDIA (*who has an eye for romance and adores men, goes to him and shakes hands*). How do you do? (*Crosses below sofa to fire to warm her feet.*)

BRIDGET (*curtly, crossing* JENNY *to shake hands with him*). How are you? (*Then to* JENNY.) That's a terrible habit, not introducin' people. Your father was just the same. When I was your age and went out to parties with him, he'd always be leavin' me hanging in mid air, not knowing who I was talking to. (*To* DAVID.) Are you staying in the house or what?

(MICK *enters from hall carrying suitcases.*)

DAVID. I just took a walk over, that's all. My people have a farm down the road.

JENNY. Come and see your rooms. Then we'll have tea. I expect you're hungry. (*Going on to stairs.*)

BRIDGET. A farm—that reminds me, Jenny. What are all those ducks doing, walkin' about in the garden? Are they meant to be there?

JENNY. Yes, they're all right.

BRIDGET. You don't eat ducks' eggs, do you? Don't you know they're poison? A whole lot of people died in Lincolnshire the other day, from eatin' duck's eggs. It was all in the *Daily Express.* Do you put them in the cookin' too?

JENNY. They're all right, Aunt Bridget. We've used them for years. (*Switching on stairs light as she goes.*)

BRIDGET. Ach, what am I to do? I shan't be able to eat a thing. (*Going upstairs.*)

JENNY. Coming, Aunt Lydia?

LYDIA. I'll just stay here and thaw for a moment, darling. I'm frozen to the bone.

JENNY (*leaning over banisters in arch*). David, do you mind tidying up a bit?

BRIDGET (*to* MICK). Remember—that's fragile.

(*They all three go out upstairs.* DAVID *pushes round sofa so that it is at right angles to the fire.*)

LYDIA (*with her back to fire; always glad, even at her age, to be alone with a man*). Isn't Jenny a darling? I'm *so* fond of her. She was so *splendid* all through my sister's illness. And now I think she's *quite* wonderful the way she looks after her father, don't you?

DAVID. Ay, she's wonderful all right, a bit too wonderful, if you ask me.

LYDIA (*puzzled by his tone*). Too wonderful? What do you mean?

DAVID. Well, in my opinion you can carry self-sacrifice a bit too far.

LYDIA (*looking at him closely, then jumping to her favourite conclusion*). Oh, . . . oh, I see. . . . Oh, I'm so glad, so *very*

glad. You're in love with her, aren't you? No, no, don't
tell me. There's no need. I can see you are. It's written
all over you. Oh, I'm *so* glad. Darling Jenny, I was so
afraid her being at home would mean . . .

DAVID. Aren't you rather jumping to conclusions?

LYDIA. Well, but I'm not wrong, am I? Don't tell me I'm
wrong. No, no, of course not. I'm never wrong about
these things. I *always know.*

DAVID. That must be a wee bit disconcerting for your
friends.

LYDIA. You're not offended, are you?

DAVID. No, I'm not offended. But we've not announced
anything yet. The engagement's not been made public.

LYDIA. But I'm not the public. Secrets of this sort are
perfectly safe with me. Oh, I *do* congratulate you. Jenny's
such a darling. This is absolutely right, I can see that.
You're cut out for each other. I can always tell.

DAVID. Are you psychic or what?

LYDIA. Oh, what a delicious Scotch voice! My husband was
Scotch, you know, from Argyllshire. And ever since my
marriage I've felt myself in a way to *be* Scotch. . . . What
part of Scotland do you come from?

DAVID (*going up into recess to get sofa table which is under window
up* L.). Not far from Aberdeen.

LYDIA. And what do you do?

DAVID. What do I do?

LYDIA. Didn't I hear you say you were a farmer?

DAVID. That's my father. He's just bought a farm down here.
I'm an engineer. (*Bringing down sofa table and placing it
above sofa.*)

LYDIA (*disappointed*). Oh, . . . I'm afraid that means nothing
to me. Engineering always seems a little—well, inhuman
somehow. I mean, it's *people* that count, isn't it? Not
material things . . . not tunnels and bridges and
machines . . .

DAVID. People often find tunnels and bridges and machines quite useful, you know.

LYDIA. Yes, but you know what I mean, don't you? After all, it's not petrol and oil that makes the world go round, is it?

(MICK *runs through from upstairs.*)

MICK. Richard and Margaret are here!

LYDIA. Were they on the train? We never saw them.

MICK. No, they've come by car. (*Goes out to front door.*)

(BRIDGET *and* JENNY *come down stairs.*)

BRIDGET (*coming to below grandfather chair*). Ach, good gracious, I don't know what to do. Is there a train back to London?

JENNY (*from stairs*). But, Aunt Bridget, really . . . we've all eaten ducks' eggs for twenty years.

BRIDGET (*turning to her*). That makes no difference. I don't see why I should be made to eat ducks' eggs if I don't want.

(JENNY *goes out to study.* RICHARD WYNDHAM *comes in followed by* MICK. RICHARD *looks much younger than his years, not only because he has the upright bearing of the professional soldier, but because he has the perennial youthfulness—or pickled adolescence—of the generation that fought in the 1914 war. He has a great air of being tough and cynical; a man's man; and treats most people and things with humorous mockery.*)

RICHARD. Brrrr . . . it's damn cold. Leave the car till afterwards, Mick. (*Coming to* R. *of* BRIDGET *and shaking hands with her.*) Hullo, Bridget, still flying off the handle?

(MICK *enters carrying his bag and takes it upstairs.*)

BRIDGET. Ach, why must you always be mockin' at people like that?

(RICHARD *crosses to shake hands with* LYDIA, R. *end of sofa.*)

RICHARD. Hullo, Lydia, how's the headache?

LYDIA (*bewildered*). Headache? I haven't got a headache.

RICHARD. Nonsense. You always have a headache.

LYDIA. Richard, dear, this is Mr. Paterson. A friend of Jenny's. Colonel Wyndham.

RICHARD (*going up to* R. *of* DAVID *to shake hands with him*). How do you do? Brrr . . . it's cold enough for snow. A hundred and forty-eight miles in an open car's no joke on a day like this. (*Taking off overcoat, which* DAVID *puts on* R. *end of sofa.*)

(JENNY *comes in from study to foot of stairs.*)

JENNY. Richard!

RICHARD (*going to* L. *of her*). Hullo, Jenny, my dear. (*They kiss each other.*) Nice to see you. How are you?

JENNY. I'm all right, thank you. Where's Margaret?

RICHARD. Margaret? Oh, she . . . er . . . she couldn't come.

JENNY. Couldn't come? Why not?

RICHARD. Not feeling very well. Touch of 'flu, I think. Thought it was better to stay put. She sent her love to you all and wished you a merry Christmas.

JENNY. Oh, dear, Daddy'll be so disappointed. He's been so looking forward to her coming . . . oh, well, there it is. Let's have some tea. (*Crossing up between* BRIDGET *and* DAVID *to* C.)

DAVID. In that case, I think I'll be getting along now, if you don't mind.

JENNY. Aren't you going to stay for tea?

DAVID. I think I'd better be getting home. The folks are expecting me.

JENNY. All right, then, David.

DAVID (*crossing below them to door*). I'll be takin' a walk over to-morrow sometime. Good-bye. (*Turning at door.*) Good-bye, all.

ALL. Good-bye, good-bye.

(DAVID *goes.* JENNY *follows towards door. As soon as he has gone,* LYDIA *pounces.*)

LYDIA (*crossing to* JENNY *down* R.). Jenny, darling, he's charming. Absolutely *charming.* I'm so glad. (*Kisses her.*)

RICHARD. Is that the boy friend?

BRIDGET (*dropping down to* R. *of sofa and to* L. *of* RICHARD). Ach, why didn't you tell me? I'd no idea of that. Congratulations.

JENNY. No, no, please. What on earth do you mean, Aunt Lydia? What's David been telling you? He'd no right to say anything.

LYDIA. He didn't. I guessed. Somehow I always know these things. He's *absolutely* right for you, my darling. Absolutely right.

BRIDGET. D'ye know, Jenny, I thought you'd never get married. Like meself.

JENNY (*suddenly desperate; to downstage of them, facing them, back to audience*). No, no. Listen, please, all of you. You're not to say a word about this to anyone. Do you see? Not to anyone.

(*Pause. Everyone is startled.*)

BRIDGET. Is he married already, or what?

JENNY (*impatiently, crossing to* R. *of* BRIDGET, *between her and* RICHARD). Of course not. It's simply that things are rather difficult at the moment. In a month's time, David's got to go abroad. He'll be away for five years. Naturally, I want to go with him. But we can't be married until I've found someone to come and look after father.

BRIDGET. Ach, that was the way with me. There was I, stuck in that little flat in West Hampstead lookin' after me invalid mother, till I was forty-five and me figure quite gone. In my opinion, parents have no right to batten on their children like that.

c

(GREGORY *comes in from front door. He is just back from the school treat, a little flustered to have kept them all waiting.*)

GREGORY. Ah, now, you've not been waiting tea for me, have you? (*He goes to* LYDIA, R. *of her. She kisses him.*)

LYDIA. Martin dear, *how* are you?

GREGORY. I'm all right, thanks. I'm sorry I'd to be out like this. Did Jenny tell you? How's Bridget? (*Crosses to her and kisses her.*)

(BRIDGET, *embarrassed, turns away muttering* " Ach! " *and goes to fireplace.* MICK *is heard whistling as he comes sauntering along the passage and downstairs.*)

Hullo, Richard. Will your car be all right out there? It's bitterly cold. (*Seeing* MICK *on stairs and crossing to him;* LYDIA *has dropped down* R. *so as not to mask them.*) Why, Mick! But I thought you couldn't get leave.

JENNY (*laughing*). He wangled it.

RICHARD. Trust him.

GREGORY. That's fine. That's fine. (*Slight pause while he looks round.*) Where's Margaret?

(*Pause.*)

JENNY. She's not coming, Daddy. (*Pause.*)

GREGORY (*crosses to* JENNY). Not coming! (*To* RICHARD.) I thought you were driving her down. Wasn't that the arrangement?

JENNY. She's got 'flu.

GREGORY. Ach, good gracious. That'll be awkward. She's all by herself there in that flat.

BRIDGET. I thought she was living with some friends of hers— married people—up in Highgate.

JENNY. She left there ages ago, Aunt Bridget.

GREGORY (*turning to* RICHARD, *now on his* R.). Did you see her this morning, Richard?

RICHARD. Yes.

GREGORY. Was she in bed?

RICHARD. When I saw her, she was all dressed up and ready to come. But she was feeling a bit off colour and thought perhaps she'd better not.

BRIDGET. Had she seen a doctor?

RICHARD. No need. It's only 'flu.

BRIDGET. That's an ignorant remark. There's more deaths from 'flu than anything else. Ach, you ought not to have left her like that. How did you know it was 'flu, anyway? It might have been rheumatic fever.

JENNY. Don't worry, Daddy. She'll be all right.

GREGORY. I don't like her to be ill there all alone. She's no one there to look after her. You'd better all go in and start your tea. Hang these things up for me, Mick. I think I'll just ring her up and see how she is. (*Moves towards stairs, on to first step.*)

> (MICK *takes his coat, hat and scarf towards hall and stays above* LYDIA.)

RICHARD. I shouldn't do that, if I were you.

GREGORY (*coming back off first step to* R. *of* RICHARD). You wouldn't? Why not?

RICHARD. There's no one else to answer the 'phone. You don't want to get her out of bed.

MICK. Hasn't she got a 'phone by her bedside?

RICHARD. Well, she might be asleep. Don't want to wake her up, do you?

JENNY. Leave it for the moment, Daddy. Come on. Let's go and have tea. (MICK *takes* GREGORY'S *coat, etc., into hall.*) I expect you're all famished. We're having tea in the dining-room; it's easier. We can think what to do about Margaret afterwards.

> (*They all begin to move up to dining-room.* LYDIA *first, up* C., BRIDGET L. *of sofa, then* RICHARD *allows* GREGORY *to cross him and up.*)

LYDIA (*as she goes*). How lovely you've made it all look, darling. So like your mother . . .

BRIDGET (*as she goes*). Is there a fire in there or shall I need me coat?

(*They are all going into the dining-room, JENNY and RICHARD last. JENNY stops up L. of recess; RICHARD C. of recess.*)

JENNY (*to RICHARD*). What about your car? Will it be all right?

(MICK *returns from hall to* R.C.)

MICK. Shall I go and put it away? It's freezing hard.

RICHARD. Don't bother. I'll do it. You go and have your tea. (*Takes his coat, etc., from R. end of sofa to hall stand, hangs up coat, goes out through door.*)

(MICK *is just going into the dining-room.*)

JENNY. Mick. Wait a moment. (*She goes to dining-room door.*) Aunt Lydia, do you mind making the tea? The kettle's on the hob. I'm just going to make up the fire. (*She shuts the door and comes to* C.) Oh lord, now I've done it again.

MICK (*by stairs* R.). Done what again?

JENNY (*coming down* R.C., *and picking up chair with box of decorations on it;* L. *of it*). Upset Bridget. I suppose I ought to have asked *her* to make the tea. Mick, what was all that upstairs about the suitcase?

MICK (*comes* R. *of her, takes chair from her; she retains the box*). Nothing. I simply made a joke, that's all. She's insufferable. She goes off the deep end for no reason at all.

JENNY. What on earth had you said? (*Putting box on sofa table and going round above sofa to fire.*)

MICK. I simply said it looked a bit precarious. It was all tied together with string.

JENNY (*amused*). Well, darling, that's fatal. (*She goes round* L. *of sofa to below it, takes pouffe off it, puts it below it towards* R. *end, takes firestool off it, puts it in front of fire and kneels to put logs on fire.* MICK *puts chair in* L. *corner of recess between windows.*)

MICK. Why? What do you mean?

JENNY. Well, you know how sensitive she is about being poor. That journey down, with Lydia behaving like an exiled grand duchess, was obviously a bad beginning for her. She was banging away in self-defence, as soon as she arrived here. I think she thinks we don't want her.

MICK. She'll be right if she's not careful . . . (*Coming down* C. *indignantly.*) I put the suitcase down and she rounds on me and calls me a cad. (JENNY *collapses in smothered laughter.*) Oh, yes, she's funny; but it's a bit much.

JENNY (*laughing*). I'm not laughing at *her*. I'm laughing at *you*. It's so funny you should *mind* being called a cad. Come on, we must go. Leave that light on, will you? (*She goes towards dining-room.*)

> (MICK *and* JENNY *go into dining-room,* MICK *turning out all lights except one lamp on table below dining-room doors and shutting dining-room doors.*
>
> *After a few moments* MARGARET *comes in at front door. She is a year or two younger than* JENNY. *She looks tired and a little strained. She puts down her suitcase by* R. *end of sofa, looks round room and sighs. She goes over to dining-room doors and listens. There is a burst of laughter from inside. She hesitates and seems unable to make up her mind to go in; then she catches sight of the whisky on table by dining-room doors; at once she snatches up bottle and pours herself out half a glass and comes down with it to above sofa. Before she has time to drink it,* RICHARD *comes in.*)

RICHARD (*stopping dead in hall opening*). Margaret! (*He goes swiftly to* R. *of her, takes away her drink, puts it back on drinks table, below dining-room doors.)* What the hell are you doing here? I thought you weren't coming. Here have I been doing my best to explain it away. Telling them some damn story about your having 'flu . . .

MARGARET. I couldn't stand it, Richard. Alone there in the flat. As soon as you'd gone I realized I couldn't stand it. A whole dreary Christmas of trekking round the pubs . . . I had to come. *(Picks up her drink again.)*

RICHARD. Well, leave that alone, anyway. You can't start your drinking here.

MARGARET. Richard, I must. I can't face them without it. When I came in just now and saw this room and heard them all talking in there, I suddenly felt I couldn't stand this either.

RICHARD. Well, what on earth *do* you want?

MARGARET. I don't know. That's the trouble. Nothing's any good. *(Drinks; he firmly takes her glass away.)* No, Richard, please . . .

RICHARD *(putting his hands on her shoulders and turning her to face them).* Come on, now. Pull yourself together.

(He goes up to the dining-room and opens the doors. MARGARET takes off her hat and crosses below him to the door. The family's conversation is broken by a cry from JENNY.)

JENNY *(off).* Margaret!

(There is a burst of general welcome into which MARGARET walks.)

CURTAIN.

THE END OF ACT ONE.

ACT II

After dinner the same evening. JENNY *is pouring coffee at the coffee tray on the sofa table. The others all come in from the dining-room, talking;* BRIDGET *and* RICHARD *are in the middle of an argument.* MICK *comes above* JENNY *and sits on the back of the* R. *end of the sofa.* BRIDGET *enters next, and coming down* C. *and round* R. *end of sofa, sits* C. *of sofa.* LYDIA *follows in to* C., *by* R. *end of sofa.* RICHARD *comes to grandfather chair and pushes it down from corner by Christmas tree to its position* R.C. MARGARET *last, closes dining-room doors and lingers in recess, smoking a cigarette.*

BRIDGET (*to* RICHARD *as they come in*). Ach, why must you always be mockin' and jeering at everything? That's what I don't understand. There's no reason at all why Socialists should be common people.

RICHARD. Common! You're no socialist, Bridget—you're just a snob.

(*Everyone laughs.* GREGORY *goes straight through and up to study.*)

JENNY. Coffee, Aunt Bridget?

BRIDGET. Thanks. White, please.

JENNY (*to* MICK, *who is waiting beside her to hand round cups*). The white owl's back again. I saw him fly across from the wood when I went to shut up the ducks.

BRIDGET (*to* RICHARD). I suppose you despise a man who earns his own living. Do you?

JENNY. Aunt Lydia?

LYDIA. White. Darling, how do you manage it all?

BRIDGET (*to* RICHARD). I think it's horrible to look down on the working classes. It's the opposite way with me. I despise people with private incomes.

LYDIA (MICK *gives her coffee and she crosses and sits in chair below fire*). Bridget, dear, need we despise anyone?

RICHARD. Bridget must. She's Irish.

BRIDGET. That's nothing to do with it. I despise the Irish more than anybody.

JENNY. Coffee, Richard?

RICHARD. Thank you, Jenny. (*Takes cup from her and goes up* C.)

MICK. What's wrong with the Irish, Aunt Bridget?

BRIDGET. What's wrong with them? Pretty well everything's wrong with them. I was glad to shake the dust of Ireland off me feet. It's a country of gamblers and drunkards.

(MICK *sits on pouffe below sofa* L.C.)

JENNY. Margaret?

MARGARET (*coming down*). Please. Black. (*Takes coffee and sits in grandfather chair* R.C.)

(*Pause.* GREGORY *comes back from study with a box of cigars, above grandfather chair to* R. *of* RICHARD.)

GREGORY. Here we are now, Richard. Do you care for cigars at all? Will you try one of these?

RICHARD. Thanks. I will. (*Takes one.*) What are they?

GREGORY. What's this they're called now? (*Crossing* RICHARD *to* C., *to get light of chandelier ; reads from inside of lid.*) Romeo y Julieta. Tabacos Habaños Genuinos. They should be all right, eh? The only trouble is they may be a bit dry. One of me churchwardens gave them to me a couple of years ago and they got mislaid in me desk.

JENNY (*laughing*). That desk! (*Giving coffee to* GREGORY.) We were excavating it the other day. If you dig deep enough you come on whole buried civilizations. We found relics of all his old parishes, right back to the beginning. (*Sitting on* L. *arm of sofa with her coffee.*)

GREGORY (*chuckling*). D'ye know we found over a thousand old sermons.

RICHARD. Good Lord! (*Sitting* R. *end of sofa.*)

GREGORY (*coming* C. *to* R. *of* RICHARD). That's not such a great number when you come to think of it. Mornin' and evenin' every Sunday; there's fifty-two Sundays in the year. . . . You'd get through a thousand in about ten years. Well, allowing for holidays and visiting preachers, say twelve. Since I was ordained, I must have preached enough sermons to fill a hundred and fifty books . . . and I doubt if anyone's ever paid the slightest attention to them.

LYDIA. Martin *dear*, I'm sure they have. I shall always remember the one you preached soon after my Philip died: " And the man that stood among the myrtle trees answered and said, These are they whom the Lord hath sent to walk to and fro through the earth ". I always remember that because of the myrtle trees. . . . I was desperately unhappy. It was such a help to me.

GREGORY (*pause; he is embarrassed*). I'm glad, Lydia, I'm glad. (*Looking at* RICHARD's *cigar.*) Well, Richard, how's it going? Is it all right?

RICHARD. Fine.

MARGARET. I must have filled a number of books too— inadvertently—about women's clothes. It's terrifying.

MICK. Why terrifying?

MARGARET. Simply because one might have been doing something else.

BRIDGET. That's what I always wonder. Why do you write that stuff? When the world's cryin' out to be saved, there's a lot more important things to be writin' about than women's undergarments.

MARGARET. How should I save the world, Aunt Bridget?

GREGORY (*after pause*). How are you feeling now, Margaret? (L. *of her.*)

MARGARET. All right, thank you.

GREGORY. Wouldn't you be better in bed. Do you feel as if you had any fever?

MARGARET. No, I don't think so. I daresay it wasn't 'flu after all.

GREGORY. You're lookin' a bit pale, you know. You've been over-workin', that's the trouble. (MARGARET *shivers*.) Are you cold?

MARGARET. A little. It's a cold night.

GREGORY. Maybe you caught a chill in the train coming down. You'd better take a glass of whisky for it. (*Going up to table by dining-room doors*.) Ach now, Jenny, we forgot all about it. Richard never had any whisky with his dinner. (*To* RICHARD.) We got this out specially for you.

RICHARD. Oh, that's all right, Martin.

(GREGORY *pours out some whisky and hands it to* MARGARET.)

MARGARET. No, thank you, father.

GREGORY. Ah, come on now, it won't hurt you. A little whisky never did anyone any harm, did it, Richard?

RICHARD. What about cirrhosis of the liver?

BRIDGET. Ach, disgusting! Is that what you've got?

RICHARD. Not yet, Bridget, not yet.

GREGORY. Come on now, Margaret, drink it up. It'll do you good.

MARGARET (*her control suddenly snapping*). Didn't you hear me say " No, thank you "?

RICHARD (*after slight pause*). Good Lord, fancy refusing a whisky. (*Rising, taking glass from* GREGORY *and going up* C.) Give it to me. I'll drink it. (*Pause;* RICHARD *drinks*.)

JENNY (*quietly, in the pause*). How bitter the holly smells . . .

(*With sigh of satisfaction* RICHARD *puts down glass*.)

LYDIA. Holly? I didn't know it had a smell.

JENNY. Yes, in the stalks. Where you break it. You know, it's in the carol: " Bitter as any gall ".

GREGORY (*moving to study above* R.). Well, I think I'll be getting along. I've some more work to do on me sermon for to-morrow.

JENNY. Don't be all the evening, will you? (*Sitting on stool in front of fire.*)

GREGORY (*moving back to* C.). D'ye know, Lydia, it's forty-two years since I preached my first Christmas sermon.

LYDIA. How old we're all getting . . .

GREGORY. To-morrow 'll be the forty-third.

LYDIA. I always think Christmas is the loveliest of the festivals.

GREGORY. D'ye know, I hate it.

LYDIA. Martin, why?

GREGORY. The brewers and the retail traders have got hold of it. It's all eating and drinking and giving each other knick-knacks. Nobody remembers the birth of Christ.

JENNY (*after pause*). But Christmas morning . . . there's something about Christmas morning . . .

MICK. In a vicarage? With services from six o'clock onwards. There's no morning at all.

JENNY. No, but the first moment, when you wake up. Somehow I don't know why—you always know it's Christmas morning. It's as if, during the night, while you were asleep, something had happened. . . . You even expect the world to *look* as different as it *feels*. And you lie there, taking it in, realizing—and that seems strangest of all—that it's Christmas everywhere.

GREGORY. Of all the sermons in the year, it's the one on Christmas morning I dislike the most. Nobody wants to hear it. They're all fidgeting in their pews, longing to be back home, basting the Christmas goose. That's no time to be tellin' them anything . . . anything important. (*Goes towards stairs, above grandfather chair.*)

JENNY. Your coffee, Daddy?

GREGORY. Coffee? Oh, ah, yes. Thank you, Jenny. I'll take it with me. (*Takes coffee from sofa table and goes out to study.*)

JENNY (*rising and going up* L. *of sofa to put her cup on sofa table*). Well, I'd better get on with the washing up. (MARGARET *gets up to help.*) Not to-night, darling. You're tired. Stay here in the warm.

LYDIA (*rising voluminously*). Can *I* be of any help?

JENNY. No, Aunt Lydia, you sit down. (*She sits again in chair below fire.*)

BRIDGET (*swiftly*). What about you, Michael? Aren't you going to help your sister?

MICK. All right, Aunt Bridget, all right. (*Rising with coffee cup and going to* L. *of sofa.*)

BRIDGET. I suppose you think it's beneath your dignity, do you? To help with the washing up? Being a man? Is that it? That's one good thing about the servant shortage, in my opinion. It's a good for the men of the country.

RICHARD. Come on, Mick. On fatigues. (*They both go out through dining-room.*)

JENNY. There's plenty more coffee, if you want any. (*She follows them out.*)

(*Pause.* MARGARET, *faced with the prospect of being left alone with the Aunts, puts out cigarette in the ashtray on the sofa table and goes to fetch a magazine from the cupboard above the fireplace and sits with it in* L. *corner of sofa. The Aunts glance at her, then at each other, and decide to attack.* BRIDGET *rises and comes round* R. *end of sofa to put down her cup on sofa table. They exchange another look.*)

LYDIA. Jenny's wonderful, isn't she?

MARGARET. Yes, I suppose she is—in a way.

LYDIA. She's so splendid with your father. I can't think what he'd do without her.

MARGARET. Let's hope he won't have to . . . "Rough, tweed shirts " . . . I never wrote that.

LYDIA. But Margaret dear, suppose Jenny wanted to get married, what would happen then?

MARGARET. She'd have to go, of course.

LYDIA. But what would become of your father?

MARGARET. Mm, I know. It'd be tiresome for him. But still, there it is. He'd have to manage somehow.

BRIDGET. Ach, what do you mean? There's no reason why you shouldn't come home, is there? (*Going to sit in* R. *corner of sofa.*)

MARGARET. No, Aunt Bridget, I'm afraid that'd be impossible —quite impossible.

LYDIA. But, Margaret, your father's so very fond of you. . . . You're the obvious person. Who else is there?

MARGARET. Look here, Aunt Lydia, what *is* all this? Jenny's not going to be married. So what's the point?

BRIDGET. The point is you've no sense of responsibility. You can't go on leaving everything to your sister like this. Look at all she does—slavin' away, runnin' this great house, without any help, and cookin' all the meals.

MARGARET. Jenny doesn't mind that. She's the domestic type.

BRIDGET. And what type do you consider yourself? The intellectual?

MARGARET. One regards oneself as an individual, Aunt Bridget. Types are other people.

LYDIA. But surely Jenny's not a type? She always seems to me to be such a very real person.

MARGARET. Everyone's a real person, Aunt Lydia. The trouble is they don't always seem so. To me Jenny's always seemed a little too good to be true. (*Pause.*) I suppose the truth is I never really feel quite at home with people who are good. Unless I can find a cosy little vice in them somewhere, they rather frighten me.

BRIDGET. I shouldn't have thought you'd be frightened of anyone.

MARGARET. Most people have vices, Aunt Bridget.

LYDIA. But you can't be frightened of Jenny, surely? She's always so simple and natural.

MARGARET. Exactly. It's that clarity of hers. It's very disturbing.

BRIDGET. I don't see what all this has to do with it. (*Putting down cup on sofa table behind her.*)

MARGARET. To do with *what*, Aunt Bridget?

BRIDGET (*confused*). Well . . . what we were talkin' about. (*Making it worse.*) Jenny slavin' away here, losin' all her opportunities . . .

MARGARET. *What* opportunities?

BRIDGET. Well, the opportunities . . . (*Rising and crossing to foot of stairs.*) Ach, I'm going upstairs now to get me work-bag. Anyway, it's a matter of principle. You wouldn't understand *that*, I suppose.

LYDIA. Bridget dear, while you're up there, I wonder if you'd mind getting mine, too?

BRIDGET (*pursing her lips*). Where is it?

LYDIA. Well, wait a minute now. I'm not quite sure. Did I unpack it or didn't I? If I didn't, it'll be in the smaller of the two brown suitcases.

BRIDGET. I don't like to be disturbin' all your things.

LYDIA. That's all right, Bridget. You'll find the key in the little key-case on my dressing table—it'll be the larger of the two short keys on the smaller of the two rings. (*Rising.*) Wait a moment, I think that's wrong. . . . Oh, dear, perhaps I'd better come and get it myself. (*Crossing and following* BRIDGET *upstairs.* BRIDGET *switches on stairs light.*)

> (MARGARET, *left alone, goes to drinks table and is about to pour out whisky when she hears* JENNY *coming and stops quickly.* JENNY *comes in through dining-room to collect coffee cups. She goes down* L. *of sofa to take* GREGORY'S *cup from below fire and then* BRIDGET'S *from* R. *end of sofa and puts them on tray on sofa table.*)

JENNY. Finished with the coffee things?

MARGARET. Yes.

JENNY. Mick's become wonderful at washing up. He's developed an army technique.

MARGARET. Jenny . . . is anything wrong?

JENNY. Why?

MARGARET. I've just sustained a combined attack from both the aunts.

JENNY. What about?

MARGARET. You. They seem to think you're fed up with being at home. That's not true, is it?

JENNY. Why shouldn't it be true?

MARGARET. Then it is. You *are* fed up.

JENNY. Not exactly, no, but . . .

MARGARET. Of course it's a preposterously inconvenient house, but I always thought you liked being here.

JENNY. So I do, very much, in a way. But it's also a bit . . . limiting, especially when . . . oh, we can't talk now. I'll tell you later. (*Picks up tray of coffee cups.*)

MARGARET (*stopping her*). Look here, Jenny, what *is* all this?

JENNY. Well, it's perfectly simple. I . . . I want to get married, that's all. (*Puts tray back on sofa table.*)

MARGARET. Darling! Who? Anyone I know?

JENNY (*coming down to* C.). He's called David Paterson. His parents have bought Copper Hall Farm. They're Scottish. He's an engineer. I expect you'd think him very dull.

MARGARET. Why should I? (*Coming down to level with* JENNY *on her* R.)

JENNY. Oh, I don't know . . . what's it matter anyway? The point is he's got a job in South America. He sails in a month's time and I want to go with him.

MARGARET. What's to prevent you?

JENNY. Who's to look after Daddy?

MARGARET (*crossing* JENNY *to fireplace*). You can always get somebody in. "Widow with small son to educate. Housework for houseroom . . ." there must be plenty of people about.

JENNY. How can I leave him with just anyone? . . . Of course, I know the perfect solution—for him.

MARGARET. What?

JENNY. You . . . Margaret, couldn't you come home for a
bit? You're such a special person to him that it would make
all the difference.

MARGARET. No. I'm sorry. That's out of the question.

JENNY (*after slight pause*). Just like that . . . yes . . . I don't
know why I asked you, really. I knew it'd be no use. All
the same . . . I don't know . . . you say it so coolly, so
immediately. Flick! Like that—and it's done with. Life
must be very easy for people like you.

MARGARET. Life's always easier than people like you make
it.

JENNY (*after pause*). You have grown hard, haven't you? No
feelings left . . . you're *armoured*.

MARGARET. Is that how I seem to you? You lack perception.

JENNY (*quickly*). I don't. I don't lack perception. (*Sitting on*
R. *arm of sofa, facing her.*) Oh, Mag, what's happened to
you? You've changed. You never used to be like this.
You must know you've changed.

MARGARET. Of course. What do you expect? Life does
change people.

JENNY. Why do you never come home? After mother died,
I made sure you'd try and come more often; but you don't.
If anything, I think you come even less. Whether you're
fond of Daddy or not, I should have thought . . .

MARGARET. Not fond of him? Do you really think I'm not
fond of him?

JENNY. Well, if you are, why is it so absolutely out of the
question that you should come home? Even if it was only
for a little while. It needn't be permanent. But there'd be
time then to look round for someone really suitable.

MARGARET. I'm sorry, Jenny. I can't.

JENNY. But why? That's what I don't understand. Why?

MARGARET. Because it wouldn't work. I don't belong here
any more. As you say, I've changed. Though perhaps not
quite in the way you think.

JENNY (*after pause, rising*). Mag, you're not happy, are you? That's it?

MARGARET. Who is ?

JENNY. Plenty of people.

MARGARET. Perhaps. If they're stupid enough.

JENNY. Oh, why must you always crackle like ice? What's happened to make you seem all frozen over inside? You're like someone out of a Hans Andersen story. Do you remember how they used to frighten me when we were small? People like the frozen queen who went down to the gardens of the dead?

MARGARET. Jenny! You're fantastic. How do you do it?

JENNY. Something has happened. I'm beginning to see now. . . . Oh, Mag, tell me. (*Kneeling on stool facing her.*)

MARGARET (*after pause*). All right, I will tell you. (*Pause, she goes* L. *of sofa to get cigarette from box on sofa table and lights it.*) You remember Bob?

JENNY. Your American? (*Sitting on firestool facing* MARGARET.)

MARGARET. My American . . . yes.

JENNY. But I thought he was killed ages ago—back in the middle of Korea. You don't mean to say he's turned up again?

MARGARET. No. He was killed. Quite, quite killed. Do you think I might have a drink?

JENNY. Of course.

MARGARET (*goes to drinks on table below dining-room doors, pours herself a stiff drink*). I was very much in love with him. You didn't know that, did you? (*Comes back to sit down* R. *of sofa.*) They found his body. What was left of it.

JENNY (*after pause*). Darling . . . why ever didn't you come home for a bit? You needn't even have told us a thing about it, but . . . oh, you *should* have come!

MARGARET. When I was pregnant? (JENNY, *unable to speak, sits very still.*) It was all rather difficult. I didn't know quite what to do. It was just about then that mother was

D

ill for the first time, you remember? I couldn't very well
tell anybody.

JENNY. You could have told me.

MARGARET. Yes. I suppose I could. But there didn't seem
any point in that. Luckily I was away in London. I
thought I'd better go through with it by myself.

JENNY. Darling. How awful for you.

MARGARET. It wasn't so bad. (*Pause.*) Once I'd made up my
mind.

JENNY. But what happened? Were you all right?

MARGARET. Quite all right. (*Another pause.*) It was a boy.
I called him Simon. I don't quite know why.

JENNY. Oh, Mag, if only I'd known . . . I see it all now.

MARGARET (*drinks and begins to talk more easily*). It was a bit
of a problem at first to know what to do with him. It's not
so easy as you might think to conceal a child. That's why
I went to live with Sally and Christopher in Highgate. They
had a Nannie for the twins. She looked after Simon, too.
That left me free in the day-time to take a job. Now you
see why I never wanted to stay here very long, when I
came. I was always wanting to get back to Simon.

JENNY (*rising, pulling pouffe up to* L. *of* MARGARET *and sitting on
it*). Of course. Oh, Mag darling, it's wonderful. I'm
longing to see him. How old is he now?

MARGARET. He'd have been five last September.

JENNY. Would have been?

MARGARET. He died last year. Meningitis. (*Finishes her drink.*)

JENNY (*gasps*). Oh . . .

MARGARET. Well, there it is. Now you know.

JENNY. Meningitis . . . and he was only four . . . when I was
in hospital, I heard a child once . . .

MARGARET (*cutting her short*). How unpleasant for you.

JENNY (*flushes*). But, Margaret . . . I don't understand.
Simon was the reason for your not coming home. But
well . . . now there's no reason left surely?

MARGARET (*rising, going round* R. *of sofa to* C.). Oh, yes there is. I couldn't stand the pretence.

JENNY. Pretence? Why need there be any?

MARGARET. Because father thinks of me as someone I no longer am. I *am* what has happened to me.

JENNY. Does it make so much difference?

MARGARET. Nothing is left the same. It's not numbness, it's not despair. It's a kind of clarity. Not like yours, though . . . because of it I just don't feel or think as I used to about *anything* in the world . . . even the little ordinary things; Christmas decorations, holly . . . Don't you see, if I lived here with father, I should have to be playing a part all the time? Pretending to be as I used to be. Never for a moment could I be myself . . . it would be an impossible, unbearable situation. The only solution would be to tell him . . . and I couldn't do that, could I?

JENNY. Couldn't you? . . . No . . . no, I suppose not. At least . . . No, I don't really see how you could. Besides it would upset him dreadfully.

MARGARET. Exactly. That's the trouble. He'd see it as a moral issue and I don't.

JENNY. Oh, if only . . . But no, we can't. Besides the whole thing's over and done with now.

MARGARET. Over and done with . . . yes . . . what nonsense life is.

JENNY. (*Slowly.*) Yes.

MARGARET. For you, too!

JENNY. Just at this moment . . . yes.

(MICK *and* RICHARD *come in from dining-room.*)

MICK (*in mock cockney*). 'Ere, 'ere, 'ere, what's all this? Skrimshanking, disgraceful, dodging fatigues.

(JENNY *rises and goes to sofa table to pick up coffee tray.* MARGARET *crosses to* R. *of grandfather chair* R.C. MICK *sits on* R. *arm of sofa,* RICHARD *goes up into* L. *of recess.*)

JENNY (*picking up coffee tray*). Sorry. I was just coming.

RICHARD. My dear Jenny, we've finished. Here give me those.

JENNY. No, no I'll do them. You've done enough for one day. Mick, could you go and get in a few logs?

MICK. Haven't *I* done enough for one day?

    (RICHARD *comes down* L. *of sofa to stand back to fireplace.*)

JENNY. No, Mick, you haven't.

MICK. O Lord, I don't see the *point* in coming home for Christmas. (*Goes out, following* JENNY *into dining-room.*)

MARGARET. I've just been telling Jenny.

RICHARD. Not about Simon? (*She nods.*) Good Lord. How did she take it?

MARGARET. Very well. There's a lot to be said for Jenny. (*Goes to refill her glass at table by dining-room doors.*)

RICHARD. Margaret, you must leave that alone.

MARGARET. No, Richard. I've got to get through the evening somehow.

RICHARD. But not that way.

MARGARET. How else? How else?

RICHARD. If you're going to start drinking, you'd much better have stayed in London.

MARGARET. Oh, well, all right. I'm sorry. I suppose I'm being rather a bore.

RICHARD. M'm, you are rather. That's the trouble with drunks, they are boring.

MARGARET. I'm not a drunk.

RICHARD. You're well on the way to being one.

MARGARET (*sitting on* R. *arm of sofa*). Nonsense Richard. Don't be silly.

RICHARD. All right. Perhaps not—yet. But how many times in the last two years have you gone to bed really sober?

MARGARET. Oh, well, in London, that's different. One has to drink in my job.

RICHARD. If that's all it is, the solution's simple. Give up the
job. Get out of London. If I were you, I'd come home.

MARGARET. That's *not* a very bright suggestion.

RICHARD (*looking at her*). Isn't it? . . . Well, you'd better
knock it off for a bit. I've never seen you quite like this
before—unable to face anything without it.

MARGARET. It's only because I *am* at home.

RICHARD. M'm. (*Pause.*) Do you know, I believe, really,
you *want* to come home?

MARGARET (*rising and going* R., *furious*). Oh, leave me alone,
Richard, for God's sake! (*Then suddenly, quietly.*) I'm
sorry. You're right, of course. But how can I? How
can I?

RICHARD. You'll only be happy when you can. (*Sitting* L. *of
sofa.*) Look here, Margaret, you're drinking on and off all
day with your Fleet Street friends; and most days you
manage to pick up one or two invitations to go out drinking
all the evening with people that bore you to tears. Failing
which you go round to the local and stay there till it shuts.
Why?

MARGARET. You know perfectly well why.

RICHARD. Because you can't face going back alone to that
flat while you're still sober enough to think. Is that it?

MARGARET. Never mind, Richard. Why do you bother
about me?

RICHARD. I have to. I'm your godfather.

MARGARET. How strange you are, Richard . . . I believe you
take that godfather business quite seriously.

RICHARD (*rising and going to fireplace*). Why not? You did.
You even borrowed money for Simon on the strength of it.

MARGARET (R. *of grandfather chair* R.C.). I've always wondered
why my parents ever chose you to be a godfather. You
don't even believe in God . . . or do you?

RICHARD. I don't like the smell of hassocks, if that's what you
mean.

MARGARET. No, it's not what I mean. Richard, please, I'm
serious.

RICHARD. Why does it matter to you what I think?

MARGARET. It does matter.

RICHARD. Why?

MARGARET. Because we're very much alike. What you can
believe, I think perhaps I might be able to believe, too.
(*Advancing towards him to* c.) Tell me, Richard. Honestly.
Do you believe in God? (*Pause;* RICHARD *says nothing.*)
No, I thought not. Ah well, there it is.

(MICK *comes in from dining-room with logs in a basket.*)

MICK. The wood's all wet. The snow's blowing right in
under the roof of the coal shed.

MARGARET. Is it?

(RICHARD *goes up* L. *of sofa into recess to help him, but*
MICK *passes in front of him, puts basket above fire and puts*
some logs on fire.)

RICHARD. Here, let me help you.

MICK. No, it's all right. I'll do it. Ah, we can get near the
fire for a change. Where are the aunts?

MARGARET. Heavens knows. They went to fetch their work.

MICK Oh Lord, we're in for a jolly evening. Two hours of
cosy Yuletide. Can't you feel it closing in on us?

MARGARET (*coming to* R. *end of sofa*). Mick, let's get out of
here. Let's go to the pictures.

MICK. O.K. Suits me.

MARGARET. Come on then. Quick. (*They run out to hall and*
can be heard from there.)

MICK. I don't expect the film'll be any good.

MARGARET. Never mind. Escape, escape, that's the thing.
The foundation of all entertainment. Oh, my bag, quick.
It's on the sofa.

MICK (*running back, putting on coat, picks up bag from* R. *corner of*
sofa). I hope you've got your Keatings in here. It's a
flea-pit. (*Runs off again.*)

(*They go out, as* JENNY *comes in from the dining-room, and she sees them go.*)

JENNY. Where are they off to?
RICHARD. The pictures.
JENNY. To-night? Oh, they can't . . . Daddy'll be so disappointed. (*Goes after them as she speaks, to* C.)
RICHARD. Jenny, I wouldn't. I don't think Margaret can quite take all this to-night.
JENNY. Oh . . . oh, perhaps not.

(BRIDGET *and* LYDIA *come downstairs with their work bags.* LYDIA *switches off stair light as she passes down.*)

BRIDGET (*on stairs*). Ach, nonsense! The Irish are a different race from the Scotch altogether. There's no connection between them at all. (*Going to* R. *of grandfather chair.*)
LYDIA (*to* JENNY, *and coming above* BRIDGET *to above grandfather chair*). We've been talking about you and your dear David.
JENNY. Come here by the fire, Aunt Bridget, and get warm.
BRIDGET. No, thanks. I don't want to soften meself.
LYDIA. Darling, listen. We've been over it all most carefully. We've come to the conclusion there's only one solution.
JENNY. What is that, Aunt Lydia?
LYDIA. Your father ought to retire. (*She crosses and sits* L. *of sofa.*)

(GREGORY *comes down from study, with book in his hand, and crosses below to sit* R. *of sofa.* JENNY *takes a small table from* R. *under banisters and puts it on* R. *of grandfather chair, then takes the lamp from table at dining-room doors and puts it on it, so that* BRIDGET *can see to sew.*)

GREGORY. There now, that's done. I'm sure I don't know what they'll make of it all. I'm going to tell them a bit about the ancient origins of their Christmas customs.
BRIDGET (*below grandfather chair* R.C.). Martin, come here a moment. I want to measure me work.

GREGORY (*gets up and goes to* L. *of her, where he stands still with wan patience while she measures her work against his chest*). Most of what they do has its roots deep in the old pagan festivities . . .

LYDIA. How very interesting . . .

GREGORY. D'ye know why you put holly on the walls at Christmas time?

LYDIA. Something to do with the Druids, isn't it?

BRIDGET. Ach, no, that's mistletoe!

GREGORY. It goes right back to the old nature-worship. The struggle between the holly and the ivy. There's a lot about it here in this book. The holly was the young men and the ivy was the girls; and they'd a struggle between them who should rule the house.

BRIDGET. The holly's won in here, I see. (JENNY *switches out chandelier and bracket lights.*)

GREGORY. There's no gettin' away from it. The whole thing's only a perpetuation of the old Roman Saturnalia . . . (*He turns and disturbs* BRIDGET *with her work.*)

BRIDGET. For goodness' sake, keep still and don't be bothering me about your old Roman—whatever you call it!

GREGORY. It was the season of general licence when everything was topsy-turvy. The slaves were the masters and the masters were the slaves.

RICHARD. I think I'll come to church to-morrow and listen to all this . . . (*Sitting* R. *end of sofa.*)

GREGORY. Well, they still do the same thing in the army to-day, isn't that so? At dinner on Christmas Day, the sergeants and the officers wait on the men.

BRIDGET (*releasing him*). Thanks. (*Sits in grandfather chair.*)

GREGORY (*wandering down* R.). Everything has its roots in something else . . . in the past . . . people have no idea of it mostly. They don't realize that when they're stickin' up their holly and pullin' their crackers and deckin' themselves

out in paper caps, they're still takin' part in an ancient winter
ritual that goes back to the dawn of history . . .

JENNY. Come and sit down, darling. Here in the warm.
(*Indicating chair before fire and sitting on footstool.*)

GREGORY (*is crossing, but stops below* R. *end of sofa to turn to*
BRIDGET). What about you, Bridget? Where are you
going to be?

BRIDGET. I'm all right here, thanks. I can see to do me work.

GREGORY (*sitting in chair below fire*). Where are the other two?

JENNY. They've gone out.

BRIDGET } (*together*). {Gone out?
LYDIA   }   {On Christmas Eve?

RICHARD. Yes, they've gone to the pictures. (*Rising and
sitting in* R. *corner of sofa.*)

GREGORY (*puzzled*). To the pictures? (*Pause.*) I didn't know
there was anything interesting on . . . (*He settles down to
his book.*)

(RICHARD *begins to light a pipe—and the long quiet
evening is before them as*

THE LIGHTS FADE FOR A FEW SECONDS.

*When they fade up again it is two hours later and they are
still sitting in more or less the same positions, except that
JENNY is now sitting on the floor, leaning on the fire stool
reading a book;* BRIDGET *and* LYDIA *knitting;* RICHARD
smoking his pipe; GREGORY *reading. They are all getting a
little somnolent. For a moment or two there is no sound but
the clicking of needles.* GREGORY *turns the pages of his book.*)

LYDIA. How quiet it is.

JENNY. It's the snow, Aunt Lydia. It muffles everything.

BRIDGET. I didn't know it had been snowing.

JENNY. It's been snowing all the evening. It's quite deep out
in the yard.

(*Pause.* RICHARD *knocks out his pipe.* BRIDGET *begins
to count her stitches.*)

GREGORY. Did ye ever know the origin of the word
" beanfeast "?

BRIDGET. I did not.

GREGORY. It seems it was a feast in honour of the king of the
Bean, the traditional Christmas prince. Did you know
that?

BRIDGET. I did not.

(*Pause.* GREGORY *returns to his book.*)

LYDIA. I do think it's such a pity all these old customs are
allowed to die out. You still have your waits here, I hope?

JENNY. Yes, worse luck. They'll be here soon.

LYDIA. Oh, but Jenny, why? It's so delightful to hear them
. . . country voices drifting across the snow . . .

JENNY. Six rather sinister little boys who can't sing in tune.
They only do it for money.

LYDIA. Oh, dear, what are we coming to?

(*Pause.* GREGORY *suddenly chuckles over his book.*)

RICHARD. What's the joke, Martin?

GREGORY. Just something that tickled me here, that's all. You
know, in the Middle Ages, they'd a Feast of Fools at
Christmas time. A choirboy or a sub-deacon'd take the
part of the bishop and they'd burlesque the church service
and so on. Well, it seems they got a bit too rowdy at times,
and in 1444 the Cathedral Chapter of Sens laid down a
regulation that not more than three buckets of water must
be poured over the precentor at vespers. (*They all laugh.*)

LYDIA. But Martin, why did they do all these extraordinary
things at Christmas time?

GREGORY. Nobody knows why. One theory is that it goes
right back to the days when they were makin' the calendar.
They stuck in some extra days to fill up the gap between
the lunar and the solar year, and when they'd stuck them in,
they felt they were queer sort of days, that didn't really
exist, days on which anything might happen.

LYDIA. How strange . . . I used to feel rather like that about Christmas when I was a child . . . Perhaps it *was* something to do with the time of the year. I remember how wonderful it used to be, seeing the snow outside, finding the Christmas stockings tied to the ends of our beds . . . and all day long a strange sort of excitement . . . and then, in the evening, downstairs in the drawing room . . . dark green and glittering, the Christmas tree. Somehow Christmas never seems quite the same now. As one gets older, the magic seems to go out of things . . .

(*The grandfather clock strikes ten.*)

JENNY (*getting up*). Ten o'clock. I must go and put the kettles on. I expect the others'll be back soon. (*She goes out into dining-room.*)

LYDIA (*glances at* BRIDGET *and decides to speak*). Martin . . .

GREGORY. Wait a minute. Just listen to this. This'll amuse you, Richard. It's talkin' about the Christmas revels at Oxford and Cambridge in the seventeenth century. The authorities frowned on them because they were bad for discipline, but—this is the amusin' part–(*Reading.*) " Some grave governors mentioned the *good* use thereof, because thereby, in twelve days, they more than discover the true disposition of scholars then in twelve months before ".

RICHARD (*laughing*). Perhaps that's the point of all Christmas gatherings.

LYDIA (*pointedly*). Richard, don't you think perhaps Jenny might like a little help?

RICHARD. What? (*Then realizing he is being got rid of, laughing.*) Oh yes, all right. (*He goes out into dining-room.*)

LYDIA. Martin . . .

GREGORY. Now then, Lydia, I'm sorry. What is it?

LYDIA. Well, Martin dear, Bridget and I have been talking. We can't help feeling that perhaps the time has really come for you to think about retiring . . .

GREGORY. Ach, nonsense, Lydia. I've several years in front of me yet.

LYDIA. Of course you have, Martin dear. That's just the point. Why not have them for yourself?

GREGORY. That's all very well, but what about me work? (*Rising.*) Perhaps you don't think that's of any importance?

LYDIA. Of course I do, Martin, of course. And I know how splendid you are. You've given yourself completely to the people of this place.

GREGORY (*pause; with back to fire*). D'ye know, Lydia, I've been here fourteen years; and sometimes when I walk through the streets and look at the faces of the people, I wonder have I made any impression at all?

LYDIA. I'm sure you have, Martin. You mustn't get depressed.

GREGORY. I wonder. D'ye know, I doubt if they've any conception of what I'm here for? They think I'm paid to marry them and bury them and sign their pension papers. Like a civil servant. As if a man of any spirit'd devote his life to that!

LYDIA. I should have thought a little country town like this would have been just the place where the parson still does have a great deal of influence.

GREGORY. You'd think so, wouldn't you? That's what I thought when I came. There's the Church, a great, fourteenth century church standin' up there in the midst of the market place, the biggest building in the town. It's the centre of the place, architecturally. It ought to be the centre of the place spiritually, too. And it could be. I'm sure of that, even to-day, even now in the twentieth century, the church *can* be the centre of the life of a place. I know it can. But it's not . . . that little tin shack of a cinema they've gone off to to-night has more influence on the lives of the people here than the church has. *That's* where the people of this place get their ideas of the meaning of life, not in church.

BRIDGET. I think the clergy have no one but themselves to blame. They're a lazy lot.

LYDIA. But you can't say that about Martin. No one could have worked harder. You deserve a rest, Martin dear. You can't go on for ever. Everyone deserves a few years to himself. It's the greatest mistake to leave it too late.

GREGORY. I'd be nothing without me work.

LYDIA. But you've got so many interests. . . . Look how you enjoy poking in your old books.

GREGORY (*in a burst of irritation*). Pokin' in old books wouldn't be enough to make sense of me life. . . . It's kind of you to bother about me, Lydia, but I'd rather carry on while I can.

BRIDGET. That's all very fine and large. You've not only yourself to think about. There's Jenny, too.

GREGORY. Jenny? What about Jenny?

BRIDGET. It's no life for a girl to be stuck away here lookin' after an old man. It's time she got away and had a life of her own.

GREGORY. She's perfectly free to go if she wants to.

LYDIA. Well, but Martin, *is* she?

(JENNY *and* RICHARD *come in with tea things from dining-room and conversation stops.* RICHARD *comes first carrying the tea-tray down* C., *and puts it on fire-stool, which* LYDIA *has put in front of sofa.*)

JENNY (*following down* L. *of sofa, with kettle which she puts in fender*). Do you mean they're the same wild geese that we see here? Do they fly all the way from Ireland to China?

RICHARD (*laughing*). Via the marshes of Norfolk? I wouldn't put it beyond them. They fly immense distances. No one ever knows where they're going. That's why they always give rise to legends.

JENNY (*sitting* R. *of sofa to pour out tea*). I didn't know you'd been in China.

RICHARD. Unofficial military mission. In Manchuria. Very secret. Mostly duck shooting.

GREGORY. Jenny, is this true what your aunt Bridget's been saying? Have you been feeling that you ought to get away from here?

JENNY (*very annoyed*). Oh, Aunt Bridget, really . . .

LYDIA. Darling, we've only been trying to persuade your father that he ought to think about retiring.

GREGORY. It's no good talking about it, Lydia. In any case, I couldn't retire for another four years. (*Sitting again in his chair below fireplace.*)

BRIDGET. Why not?

GREGORY. Because of Michael.

JENNY. Tea, Aunt Bridget?

BRIDGET. Thanks. What's Michael got to do with it?

GREGORY. I want him to have a chance to find his feet in the world before I retire.

JENNY. Aunt Lydia?

LYDIA. Very weak, darling. Otherwise I can't sleep.

GREGORY. He's got this year to do in the army first. After that I want him to go to Cambridge.

BRIDGET. Ach, what's the good of sending a fellow like him to Cambridge? He'll only be wasting his time there.

LYDIA. Why should he? How *can* you say that, Bridget?

BRIDGET. Well, he's no brains, has he?

JENNY. Oh, no, Aunt Bridget, you're quite wrong. Mick's quite clever in a way.

BRIDGET. I thought at school he was never any good at anything but football. I don't approve of all this sport. It's rotting the brains of the country. (*They all laugh.*)

JENNY. Whisky, Richard?

RICHARD. Please.

JENNY. You'd better help yourself. (RICHARD *does so from table below dining-room doors.*)

RICHARD. Has Michael any idea what he wants to do?

GREGORY. I don't think he has yet, no.

BRIDGET. What's the use of his going to the University then?

GREGORY (*rising and coming to stand with his back to fire*). Don't you think it might help him to find out? It's not always easy to know what you want to do in the world, until you've been able to form some idea of what the world's about. Isn't that what a university's for?

BRIDGET. I thought it was to train people to earn their livings.

GREGORY. Ach, no! It's more than that. A university's almost the only place left where truth is valued for its own sake, not for the money it'll earn or the power it'll get you. (*Taking tea from* JENNY.)

BRIDGET. That's high falutin' talk. What does the truth, as you call it, matter to Michael?

GREGORY (*suddenly angry, crossing to* L. *of* BRIDGET, *cup in hand*). It matters to any man born, Bridget. I'll not have you saying that. About Michael or anyone else. We're all born and we've all to die; and the truth matters to all of us—the truth about what we are and what we're for—the truth about human destiny.

RICHARD (*returning to and sitting in his chair below fire*). Hear, hear. That's the stuff to give 'em.

GREGORY. You agree with me, do you?

RICHARD. Of course I agree with you. I agree with every word you said.

BRIDGET. You're not a varsity man, are you?

RICHARD. No, but I wish I had been. (*Coming down to* L. *of* BRIDGET.) Listen, Bridget, I've been a soldier all my life . . .

BRIDGET. That's nothing to boast of. I think soldiering's a low profession. I agree with the old Chinese. They classed soldiers and prostitutes as the lowest ranks of society.

RICHARD (*crossing below to fireplace and standing with his back to it*). Agreed. Soldiers are simply a regrettable necessity. Agreed. In a sane world we should do without them. Agreed. But there's nothing like life in the army to make you wonder what life is all about. (*They all laugh.*) No, no, I'm serious. Listen. I've seen a lot of fighting. From 1915-18 I was in the trenches. For three years I watched men dying all round me. Nearly all the fellows who were boys with me were killed before they were thirty. That's enough to make you wonder what the purpose of life is; that's enough to convince you that this " truth " Martin talks of is the only thing that matters.

BRIDGET. If you feel that, I wonder you ever became a soldier at all—in peace time, I mean.

RICHARD. Do you know why I did? When I was sixteen my father came to me one morning during the holidays and said: " Dick, it's time you decided what you want to do. Any preference? ". I hadn't. " Well ", said my father, " your mother and I have been talking it over; and we've decided it's a choice between two things. Which is it to be? Soldier or clergyman? " (*Pause.*) I chose to be a clergyman. My father roared with laughter, said I'd never manage the Greek. The next year, I was packed off to Sandhurst.

JENNY. Did you really want to be a parson, Richard? Seriously?

RICHARD. Well, I don't know . . . at that age . . . it's hard to say. But it seemed to me a more valuable job.

GREGORY. Most people don't think so. Would you still say that?

RICHARD. Yes, Martin, I would.

LYDIA. But, Richard, that means all your life you've been doing something you didn't really want to do.

RICHARD. That's why I'm on Martin's side over this university business. I think a fellow ought to have every chance to find out what he wants to do with his life . . . it's a bad thing to make a mistake about that . . . a damn bad thing.

LYDIA. I can't get over it, Richard. We've known you all these years, ever since you were a boy. Now I feel as if we'd never really known you at all. I've always thought of you as essentially, ideally a soldier.

RICHARD. Well, it's Christmas Eve. It's Martin's " queer time of the year ", when we all get to know each other better.

GREGORY. Of course, I don't think there's anything very remarkable about Michael. Most young fellows of his age are in the same boat—plenty of general intelligence and no particular talent . . . but that's just their problem. I often think education's more important for them than for the talented ones.

BRIDGET. Ah well, perhaps I'm wrong. I never thought of it this way.

JENNY. Another cup, Aunt Bridget.

BRIDGET (*rising and going to* R. *of sofa to give* JENNY *her cup*). Thanks, I will.

LYDIA. Listen! Isn't that the waits?

(*Very, very far away, almost inaudibly, the sound of a carol " The holly and the ivy ".*)

JENNY. They don't sound so bad a long way off.

BRIDGET (*going to above grandfather chair, listening*). What's this they're singing? I can't make it out.

(MARGARET *comes in from hall. She has been drinking heavily, but the only sign of this is her extreme pallor. For a moment she stares at them all, as if she couldn't quite take in her surroundings. There is a general cry of welcome. She stops just inside the room.*)

MARGARET. Hullo.

(RICHARD *realizes at once what is wrong with her and is silent, but the others welcome her.*)

GREGORY (*rising and putting his cup on tray on stool below sofa*). Ah, there you are. Good. Come and sit down.

JENNY. You're just in time for tea. It's still quite hot.

LYDIA. Come and get warm. You look frozen.

E

BRIDGET (*coming round* R. *of grandfather chair and sitting down to her work again, with disapproval*). Some people put films before family, I see.

GREGORY (*who has been startled by* MARGARET'S *pallor*). Now, Margaret, you're going to sit over here. And you'll take some whisky. (MARGARET *shrugs*.) I'll have no nonsense this time. (*Going up to whisky on table by dining-room doors.*) You'll be makin' yourself ill again if you go on like this.

MARGARET (*pulling off her scarf, and advancing to* R.C.). Well, Richard, had a cosy evening?

(RICHARD *looks at her and says nothing. She realizes that he knows she is drunk.*)

JENNY. Pass me the kettle, Aunt Lydia, would you?

MARGARET (*putting scarf on newel post of banisters, then starting to move across room towards* C.). Your gardens of the dead are here to-night, Jenny. With a vengeance. It's like walking over the surface of the moon. The snow . . . the snow's . . . too . . . pale . . . (*She collapses near the foot of the stairs.*)

(*General reaction.* GREGORY *turns and begins to move down with a cry of horror.*)

GREGORY. Margaret!

(BRIDGET *up from her chair, checked at once and forcefully by* RICHARD'S *voice.*)

RICHARD. Leave this to me. (*He strides across the room and bends over* MARGARET, *then says quietly.*) Jenny, come and give me a hand.

(RICHARD *crosses to below* MARGARET *and* JENNY *to above her to help him pick her up. When he has lifted her, she goes upstairs, switching on stair light, and he follows up carrying* MARGARET, *leaving the group in the room, still frozen in the same positions, aghast.*)

GREGORY.   Ah, she should never have gone out in the cold like this.   Before we know it that 'flu of hers will be turning to pleurisy.

BRIDGET.   She's drunk, Martin, that's what it is, she's drunk.

(MICK *comes in singing.*)

MICK   " The holly and the ivy
          Are both now full well grown;
          Of all the trees
          That are in the wood
          The holly bears the crown . . . "

We've just passed the waits.   They're over at David what's-his-names's . . . you know, Jenny's boy friend.   Hullo, Aunt Bridget.   Had a nice evening?   (*Kisses her.*)

BRIDGET.   Disgusting!   (*Her reaction causes* MICK *to step back a little and she goes above him and off upstairs.*)

(*Before following her,* LYDIA *crosses to* GREGORY C. *and lays her hand on his shoulder.*)

LYDIA.   Good night, Martin dear.   (*She goes out between* GREGORY *and* MICK *and upstairs.*)

MICK (*turning to watch them go, then coming to back of grandfather chair*).   Oh?   They've gone?   We had rather a bit of luck— saw rather a good film . . .   " Nanook of the North ".   (*Pause.* GREGORY *looks at him, clearly not believing him.*)   All about esquimaux . . . of course, it's old, but it's . . .

GREGORY.   You've not been near a cinema.   Why don't you tell the truth?

MICK.   The truth?   (*Then suddenly bitter.*)   You can't be told the truth, that's the trouble . . . that's the whole trouble . . . (*His whole force is behind the denunciation.*)   You can't be told the truth.

GREGORY (*after pause, turning away*).   You'd better go to bed, Michael.

(MICHAEL *goes upstairs.* GREGORY *alone, sits in grand-father chair* R.C., *thinking.   After a second or two, the waits* start up outside the house. *They are exactly as* JENNY *described them. They sing matter-of-factly the first verse of "While shepherds watched their flocks by night".* JENNY *comes downstairs while they are singing.*)

GREGORY. Go and get rid of them, Jenny. (*Feels in pocket for money.*)

JENNY. It's all right. There's a shilling here. (*Going to mantelpiece.*)

(*By now they have started the second verse. As she goes to the door they break off abruptly in the middle of a line to knock loudly on door. She gets rid of them; there is the sound of voices wishing her "Happy Christmas". She comes back to* GREGORY *and sits on* R. *arm of his chair, her* L. *hand on his* L. *shoulder.*)

GREGORY (*patting her hand absentmindedly*). Ah, Jenny, what would I do without you?

JENNY (*beside him, quietly*). You'll never have to.

CURTAIN.

THE END OF ACT TWO.

ACT III

Christmas morning. Brilliant sunshine on snow outside window. The room is bright with reflected light. The church bells are ringing.

GREGORY bursts in from dining-room, carrying a napkin. He has obviously left the breakfast table abruptly as the result of a row. He hesitates up C. and then crosses towards study, looking harassed and perplexed. JENNY follows him, closing door behind her and comes down to L. of him, as he stands on first step of stairs.

JENNY. You know what Aunt Bridget is . . . she's always like that about them both—especially Mick. It doesn't mean anything. Do come and finish your breakfast.

GREGORY. I'll not go in there again. I don't care to discuss it with them.

JENNY. But you must have something to eat. You've been up ever since six, with all the services . . . and no food. It's so bad for you.

GREGORY. I've had all I want, thanks. (*Gives napkin to her and turns towards study, stopping and turning back.*) How is Margaret this morning? Have you seen her?

JENNY. She's having breakfast in bed. I took her a tray up.

GREGORY. Is she all right?

JENNY. Yes, she's all right. (*Pause; GREGORY turns towards study, but her voice stops him.*) Need you let all this worry you so much, Daddy? Need you let it spoil the whole day? After all, it's Christmas.

GREGORY. Christmas . . . Bridget's right, though, Jenny. That is what they'll be sayin' to-day—what's the good of him and all his talk about religion? It doesn't even prevent his own children gettin' drunk . . .

JENNY. But that's all so unfair. It's not *your* fault.

GREGORY (*pause; frowns and sighs*). Perhaps it is my fault . . .
I don't know . . . (*Goes up into study.*)

> (JENNY *puts napkin on table by dining-room doors and
> rearranges the Christmas presents round the vase of honesty on
> the circular table in recess up* C. MICK *appears furtively on the
> stairs in pyjamas and dressing gown.*)

MICK (*leaning over banisters of arch on the landing*). Whist!
Jenny! Happy Christmas!

JENNY (*impatiently*). Oh, Mick . . .

MICK. What time is it?

JENNY (*coming down* C.). Nearly ten. Do hurry up and get
dressed before anyone sees you.

MICK. How is everything?

JENNY. What do you expect after last night? Bridget's
popping and sputtering like boiling fat. (MICK *laughs.*)
And Lydia's being " soothing ".

MICK (*nodding towards study*). How's he taking it?

JENNY. Well, he's a bit upset. The whole thing rather
depresses him.

MICK. Oh, Lord . . . (*Sauntering down to foot of stairs.*)
Why the hell must people always make such a fuss about
nothing?

JENNY. It's not quite nothing, Mick. Getting drunk in a pub
where everyone knows you both . . . it does Daddy so
much harm.

MICK. It's nothing to do with him.

JENNY (*going below sofa to put a log on the fire*). But people
don't see it like that. You can't expect them to really.

MICK (*advancing to* R.C.). Why not? I do expect them to.
Anyway, they can't have noticed much. I didn't. I'd no
idea she was so drunk. She didn't show any sign of it. I
was amazed when Richard told me last night that she'd
passed out.

JENNY. He thinks it was probably the cold air on the way home. Anyway, she'd had rather a tough time before she went out with you.

MICK (*to* R. *end of sofa*). She drinks like a fish, you know.

JENNY (*frowns unhappily*). Only because she's miserable.

MICK (*sitting on* R. *arm of sofa*). Yes . . . I say, what *about* all that? (JENNY *looks surprised that he knows.*) I had that last night instead of the pictures. It shook me, you know . . . (BRIDGET'S *voice is heard from dining-room.*) O Lord!

(BRIDGET *comes in from dining-room and* MICK *bolts upstairs.*)

BRIDGET (*over her shoulder to* LYDIA). That's a lot of senti-mental nonsense . . . Jenny, where do you keep your rail guide? (*Coming to* R. *of grandfather chair* R.C.)

JENNY. Our what, Aunt Bridget? (*Rising from fireplace.*)

BRIDGET. Rail guide. I'm going back to London.

JENNY. Oh, Aunt Bridget, you can't . . . (*Going up to* L. *end of sofa.*)

BRIDGET. I don't care to stay here after what happened last night. It makes everything so awkward. I never felt so uncomfortable in me life as I did just now at breakfast.

(LYDIA *comes in from dining-room and remains up* L.C.)

LYDIA. Oh, dear, the bells have stopped. I'm not nearly ready for church.

JENNY. It's all right, Aunt Lydia. That's only the first lot. There's plenty of time yet.

BRIDGET. I suppose you'll have trains runnin' from here to-day, will you?

LYDIA (*coming down* L. *of* BRIDGET). Bridget, you're *not* going?

BRIDGET. I am.

LYDIA. But it's so *wrong* to take up this attitude . . . I *do* feel it's so wrong . . . we ought to try to be more tolerant.

BRIDGET. I don't see the point of toleratin' low habits.

LYDIA. Well, after all, it's not our business. We really must leave all that to Martin, I think. Anyway, Bridget, you ought to stay, if only for Jenny's sake. She's taken so much trouble about everything and made all these wonderful preparations . . . (*She indicates the pile of presents round the vase of honesty.*) I really do think it's most unkind of you to go off like this. (*Going up to* L. *of presents' table in recess up* C. *and looking out of* L. *window.*)

BRIDGET (*abruptly rueful*). I didn't mean it that way, at all.

JENNY (*crossing above sofa to* L. *of* BRIDGET). Of course you didn't, Aunt Bridget. I know.

LYDIA (*at window*). Just look at the sun, on the snow . . . it's heavenly.

JENNY. You'll miss the goose, Aunt Bridget, if you go now . . .

BRIDGET. Goose, is it, ye're havin', not turkey?

JENNY. Oh, dear, don't you like goose?

BRIDGET. I do. I prefer it.

LYDIA (*still at window*). We might almost be in . . . in Finland, or somewhere . . . (*Turns from window to presents' table.*)

BRIDGET (*distracted with indecision about the goose*). Now I don't know what to do.

JENNY. Stay then, Aunt Bridget, please. Do stay.

BRIDGET. Very well, then. I will.

LYDIA (*pouncing on a parcel for her and unwrapping it*). Oh, I know what this is, don't I? It's larger than ever this year . . . Darling, how good of you. There's nothing in the world to touch it—real old-fashioned eau-de-Cologne. Thank you so much, darling. Let me kiss you. (*Coming down to* L. *of her.* JENNY *hesitates.*) It *is* for *me*, isn't it?

JENNY. Yes, Aunt Lydia, it is, but . . .

LYDIA. Darling, you shouldn't. It's so expensive. Though it's not really a luxury for me, of course. It's a necessity. I have such appalling headaches. I need gallons of it. Thank you so much, darling.

JENNY. It's not from me, Aunt Lydia, this year. It's from Daddy.

LYDIA. Oh, dear . . . perhaps I ought not to have opened it
yet then?

JENNY. That's all right. In fact, I think it's quite a good idea.
Let's start the presents now, shall we? Would you like
that, Aunt Bridget? I think there's time before church.

BRIDGET. As you please. I'll go and get mine then. (*She
goes upstairs.*)

LYDIA (*crossing to warm her feet at fire*). Poor Jenny. I do
sympathize. It's going to be a trying day for you, I'm
afraid. I'm so glad you persuaded her to stay.

JENNY. She's not easy, is she?

LYDIA. That comes of living alone. It's apt to make people
difficult. (*Examining cards on mantelpiece.*) Oh, what a
sweet little kitten.

JENNY (*sitting on* R. *arm of sofa*). It hasn't made you difficult,
Aunt Lydia.

LYDIA. Ah well, it's different for me. There's been someone
in my life. I've not always been alone . . . though sometimes it almost seems as if I had. . . . It's thirty-two years
since your Uncle Philip died . . . for thirty-two years—
more than the whole of your lifetime, Jenny—I've been
living in hotels, trying to take an interest in the people I
meet . . . with no one I care a rap for . . . certainly no one
who needs me. . . . Strange how our life only seems to
have meaning because of someone else. . . . You understand
that, Jenny, you're in love.

JENNY. Don't, Aunt Lydia; that's all over.

LYDIA. Jenny! What's happened? Have you seen David this
morning? (*Sitting on sofa near* JENNY *who is on* R. *arm of it.*)

JENNY. No. But we can't get married. I see that now. I
realized it quite clearly last night.

LYDIA. Oh, darling, no. That's such a mistake . . . when
you're in love, you mustn't let anything stand in your way.

JENNY. Isn't that sentimental, Aunt Lydia? Marriage isn't
the only thing in the world.

LYDIA. It's a very important one.

JENNY. Don't you think people exaggerate its importance?

LYDIA. No. I'm seventy, Jenny. I've seen quite a lot of the world. I know what I'm talking about. Everyone needs someone else. Loneliness is a terrible thing. It can do appalling things to you . . . that's why I'm always so sorry for people like Bridget. She did what you're thinking of doing. She stayed at home to look after your grandmother.

JENNY. I think she was quite right to do that.

LYDIA. Perhaps. But think what it has meant . . . Ever since your grandmother died, Bridget has been quite alone. If she died to-morrow, there's no one to whom it would really make the slightest difference . . . That's why it means so much to her to be here with you all for Christmas . . .

> (BRIDGET *comes downstairs with her parcels to below grandfather chair* R.C.)

BRIDGET. I've brought these few trifles. What shall I do with them?

JENNY (*rising and going to* L. *of* BRIDGET). Put them on the table, Aunt Bridget, with the others.

BRIDGET (*holding out a soft parcel*). That's for you.

JENNY. Oh, thank you. Thank you very much.

BRIDGET (*goes below* JENNY *up to above presents' table* C. *of recess*). Why do you have this dirty old papery stuff here? What's this they call it?

JENNY. Honesty.

BRIDGET. I don't like it. (LYDIA *rises and goes to mantelpiece.*) I brought a dictionary for Michael. I suppose he won't care for that.

JENNY. Oh, I think he would, very much.

BRIDGET. Would you? (*Passing round to* L. *of presents' table.*) It seems to me he has the mentality of a corner boy. (*Pause; then almost wistfully.*) Ach, that was horrible last night. I can't get over it somehow. It seems to have spoiled everything.

(RICHARD *comes downstairs, laden with parcels.*)

RICHARD (*cheerfully*). Morning, everyone! Happy Christmas.

JENNY. Happy Christmas.

RICHARD. What shall I do with these?

JENNY. Put them over there on the table, Richard. Then come and have some breakfast.

RICHARD (*goes below* JENNY *and up to* R. *of presents' table*). No, no, it's all right. I've had some. With Margaret. I ate hers. Had some tea out of her pot.

LYDIA. Dear Richard . . . A happy Christmas.

RICHARD. Same to you, Lydia. Happy Christmas, Bridget.

BRIDGET (*turning away impatiently to* L. *window*). Ach . . .

RICHARD. What's wrong with you?

BRIDGET. Do you think it's likely to be a happy Christmas after what happened last night?

RICHARD. Don't be silly, Bridget. That's nothing. Everyone gets tight once in a way.

BRIDGET. I don't. I consider it a low habit. You've been up there with Margaret, butterin' her up, I suppose, tellin' her it's a fine thing to get drunk.

JENNY (*who has opened her parcel*). Oh, Aunt Bridget, it's lovely. Did you make it yourself?

BRIDGET. I did.

RICHARD. What's it supposed to be?

BRIDGET (*going to* L. *of* JENNY). It's a bed cape. (*To* JENNY.) You read a lot in bed, don't you? It's to keep your shoulders warm.

JENNY. Thank you so much. (*Kisses her.*)

BRIDGET. I suppose you won't be needin' it now you're gettin' married.

JENNY. I'm not getting married. (*Puts bed cape on grandfather chair.*)

BRIDGET. What? Have you broken it off then?

LYDIA. Jenny . . . (*Stepping forward to below sofa.*)
JENNY. No, no. Please. You were never supposed to know
about David and me. It was only because Aunt Lydia was
so . . . well, so perspicacious. We're not really engaged at
all. David has asked me to marry him. But I told him I
couldn't. At least, not at present. Unless Margaret could
be persuaded to come home and look after Daddy. Well,
after last night I saw quite clearly that that's out of the
question . . .
LYDIA. Darling, it's not. You exaggerate.
JENNY (*crossing to* R. *end of sofa*). Aunt Lydia, you don't really
know. Please let me finish. When I see David to-day, I
shall have to tell him, that's all. That we can't be married.
It was never supposed to be public. It was just between
ourselves. So please forget all about it. (*Turns upstage.*)
    (MICK *comes downstairs to foot of them.*)
MICK. The snow's coming through the bathroom ceiling.
JENNY (*almost in tears*). Oh, I know that place. It only drips
in the bath.
MICK (*going to* BRIDGET). Happy Christmas, Aunt Bridget.
(*Kisses her.*)
BRIDGET. Ach! (*Turns away in disgust and steps downstage to
address* LYDIA.) Are you coming, Lydia? I'm going to get
ready for church. (*Crossing to stairs.*)
LYDIA. Yes, yes, I'm coming. (*Crossing to follow, as far as* L.
of MICK.) Dear Mick . . . Happy Christmas. (*Kisses him.*)
MICK. Happy Christmas.
    (*The* AUNTS *both go upstairs.* RICHARD *drops down* L.
of sofa to fireplace.)
JENNY (*to* MICK). The breakfast's all cold by now.
MICK. Don't want any breakfast. I feel awful. Is there any
coffee?
JENNY. There may be a little. Anyway, I'm just going to
make some more for Daddy before church. I'll bring you
some. (*Goes out through dining-room.*)

MICK (*crossing to below sofa; to* RICHARD). Margaret says will
you drive her over to Melton?   There's a train at 11.5.

RICHARD.   She's going then, is she, after all?

MICK (*sitting on sofa*).   I don't blame her.   For two pins I'd
go too.   It's going to be hell here to-day.   Got a cigarette?
(RICHARD *hands case*.)   Thank God, you're here anyway.

(JENNY *comes in with cup of coffee, which she puts on sofa
table and goes* C.)

JENNY.   Here's a cup to be going on with.   (MICK *rises and goes
between her and sofa for it*.)   I'm just going to make some
more.   Would you like some, too, Richard?

RICHARD.   I don't know if I've got time before the train.
How far's Melton?

JENNY.   What train?   You don't mean to say Aunt Bridget's
going after all?

RICHARD.   Bridget?   No.   Margaret.

JENNY.   Oh . . .   Oh, she mustn't!   (*Turning to stairs and back
again*.)   Well, I don't know . . .   Perhaps it's best . . .
Richard I don't like to talk to Daddy about it, but what
about this drinking of hers?   You see her in London.   Can't
you do something?

RICHARD.   Well, it's more or less routine, you know, in her
job.   They all do it.

JENNY.   But it was frightening last night, Richard.

RICHARD.   I shouldn't worry too much about last night,
Jenny, if I were you.   Last night was an exception.   (MICK
sits on back of sofa, R. *of sofa table*.)   After all there were . . .
special circumstances.   Coming home at all was a bit of a strain.

JENNY.   But when she came in—I've never seen her look like
that before—and then collapsed . . .

RICHARD (*sitting on fire-stool facing her*).   Now, look here,
Jenny, *passing out means nothing*.   I know what I'm talking
about.   I've spent half my life among pretty heavy drinkers.
And there's very little I don't know about alcoholism, from
the inside, as you might say.   Passing out may look terrible,

but you can't tell from that how much a person usually drinks. It might happen to anyone. In fact, the most likely sort of person to pass out after a few stiff whiskies and a walk through the snow would be someone like you, who never touches a drop.

MICK (*rising and putting his arm round her*). I'm mad to see Jenny blind.

RICHARD. No, the real danger with Margaret is that if she stays on alone in London, she'll develop a regular routine habit, and that'll be difficult to break.

JENNY (*sitting on* R. *arm of sofa*). I don't think it's quite that. I know all about Margaret . . . now. She told me last night. She only drinks because she's unhappy.

MICK (*coming down* C. *a step*). I don't blame her. It was tough enough just listening to it in the pub last night. She's had enough to make her unhappy.

RICHARD. Well, she'll have to get over that. We can't bring them back from the dead for her, can we?

JENNY. No, I don't mean that exactly. Her unhappiness isn't grief. It's . . . it's because she's askew with the world.

RICHARD. Maybe. But her . . . her . . . well, her askewness, or whatever you call it, is considerably worse than her drinking, you know. At present. I know Margaret pretty well, and I believe if she could only get some of this askewness straightened out, she'd be all right. And of course, London's the last place to do that.

JENNY. I wish she wasn't going back to the flat all by herself.

RICHARD. Now, Jenny! You mustn't get melodramatic ideas about her.

JENNY. I wasn't. I was just thinking . . . It's a bit bleak for her. To-day of all days.

RICHARD. I'll go with her if you like.

JENNY. No, no, Richard, of course not. Oh, dear, I must get on. The goose'll never be ready at this rate. (*Goes out between* MICK *and sofa through dining-room.*)

MICK (*wandering up* C.). Have you seen my father this morning?

RICHARD. Not yet, no.

MICK. The trouble is they make such a damn fuss about everything.

RICHARD. Who do?

MICK (*coming back and sitting on* R. *arm of sofa*). People like my parents. Religious people. Mother was just the same. Any conversation goes right back to the creation of the world, *and* beyond.

RICHARD. Well, why not?

MICK. Well, take a thing like last night. I was tight. I admit that. Anyone'd have the right to be a bit annoyed about that. It was damn silly, in front of the aunts and all. But an ordinary father—a stockbroker or something—would just tick you off and leave it at that. With a parson the whole thing's different. He probably won't be angry. He may not even say anything. But he'll be what Jenny calls " upset "—which is worse. And if anything *is* said, before we know where we are we'll get involved in a great argument about sin and the Bible and the existence of God . . . Oh, I don't know, it's all very difficult. . . . You see, if you don't believe what he believes, you can't very well say so, because it amounts to telling him that in your opinion his whole life is based on a fallacy . . . which is a bit rude.

RICHARD (*rising*). Never mind, Mick old boy. We'll all be dead in a hundred years. How far is this place Melton?

MICK. About twelve miles.

RICHARD (*crossing to hall*). I'd better go and see if the car will start. The roads'll be terrible. It's been snowing all night. (*Goes out through hall.*)

> (MICK, *alone, goes to parcel table,* C. *of recess.* GREGORY *comes down from study looking for* JENNY *and calling.*)

GREGORY. Jenny! . . . Jenny! (*Stopping on first step.*) Oh, hullo, Mick. D'ye know where Jenny is?

MICK. Through in the kitchen. I'll fetch her.

GREGORY. No, no. Just tell her I'm ready for me coffee, will you?

MICK. She's making it now, I think.

GREGORY. She is? Good. Good. (*Pauses, looks at* MICK, *finds conversation too difficult and turns back to study.*) Ah, well . . .

MICK (*awkwardly, coming down* C. *a little*). Father . . .

GREGORY (*frowning*). Yes?

MICK. I'm sorry about last night.

GREGORY. Well, there it is. It can't be helped now. (*Advancing to* R. *of grandfather chair.*) Tell me, do you often take too much to drink?

MICK. Not often, no. Of course not.

GREGORY. It has happened before though, has it?

MICK. Well, yes. I've been a bit tight once or twice.

GREGORY. I suppose you don't think anything of it?

MICK. Well, I suppose it's a bit silly. But I don't think it's anything very terrible. Anyway, it all depends on how tight you get.

GREGORY. Does it? It does not. That's a superficial way of looking at things. The rightness or wrongness of anything you do depends on what you think life is for. Have you never thought of it that way?

(JENNY *comes in with coffee on tray and passes* L. *of* MICK *to put it on sofa table.*)

JENNY. Everything in the larder's frozen. The milk's solid ice. (*Realizing she has interrupted.*) Oh . . . I'm sorry. (*To* GREGORY.) Here's your coffee, darling. Drink it while it's hot. (*Going back to dining-room doors.*)

GREGORY. Thank you, Jenny. I shan't want all that.

JENNY. Mick's having some too. When you've finished, Mick, come and give me a hand with the washing up.

MICK (*eager to escape, goes up* C. *as if to follow*). I'll come now.

JENNY. No, no, have your coffee first. (*Goes out into dining-room.*)

(MICK *comes down to sofa table and pours out coffee for his father.*)

GREGORY (*coming to* R. *of* MICK). Ah well, there it is. I don't want to spoil your Christmas for you. I daresay it was only an accident last night. But you might have seen to it that you didn't make your sister drunk. (*Going to below grandfather chair with his coffee.*)

MICK. *I* made her drunk! It wasn't *my* fault.

GREGORY. You're not suggesting it was hers, are you?

MICK. Well, it certainly wasn't mine. I didn't even realize she meant to go to the pub.

GREGORY (*annoyed for the first time*). Ach, don't start making excuses. What's it matter who thought of it first? That's a contemptible thing to say.

MICK. Well, but it's true.

GREGORY. I suppose you're of an age to be responsible for your own actions. Aren't you ashamed to stand there and tell me it was your sister who made you drunk?

MICK. Well but. . . the truth is . . . (*Pause, then impatiently.*) Oh, well, all right. Have it your own way.

(*They stand facing each other for a moment in silence.*)

GREGORY (*crossing below to fireplace and putting his cup on mantelpiece*). Look here, Michael. I wasn't going to say anything about this, but . . . there's something else that's been bothering me. I don't suppose you were too drunk to know what you were saying last night?

MICK. No, I wasn't.

GREGORY. Well, do you remember what you said to me when you came in here?

MICK. That we'd been to the pictures, you mean?

GREGORY. No, no. After that. I asked you why you didn't tell me the truth. Do you remember what you said then?

MICK. Yes—I remember.

GREGORY. You said that I couldn't be told the truth, didn't you?

MICK. Yes.

F

GREGORY. What did you mean by that?

MICK (*coming down* C. *a step; after pause*). Oh, . . . I don't know . . . it's all too difficult . . .

GREGORY. But I want to know. What did you mean when you said I couldn't be told the truth?

MICK. Well—I meant—exactly what I said. You can't be told the truth. At least not by us. Not by Jenny and Margaret and me. The real facts about us would upset you too much. So we lie to you. Or, at least, if we don't lie, we conceal the truth from you. The whole situation in this house is built on lies and concealment.

GREGORY (*indignantly*). Situation in the house!

MICK. Well, look at what happened just now. I was trying to tell you about what happened last night, about Margaret. But you wouldn't listen. Oh, I understand well what you meant about responsibility . . . but the plain fact is that she drinks. (*Pause;* GREGORY *turns away.*) There, you see, it does upset you. Can you blame us for trying to conceal that sort of thing?

GREGORY. How long have you known this?

MICK. Only since last night. It's just one of the things I did find out last night. (*Pacing up* C.) Oh, of course there have always been things you couldn't be told. (*Coming back to* R. *end of sofa.*) But I didn't realize how far it had gone. When it's a question of Jenny spoiling her whole life . . .

GREGORY. Jenny? What on earth are you talking about?

MICK. Only that Jenny wants to get married—to David Paterson.

GREGORY (*delighted*). Does she now? That's fine. That was me own idea. But I thought nothing was coming of it. . . .

MICK. Yes, but wait. She felt she ought not to, unless Margaret would come home and be with you.

GREGORY. Ach, there's no need for her to feel that.

MICK. Well, anyway, that's not the point. Last night she asked Margaret to come. And Margaret refused.

GREGORY (*silent for moment, then*). I don't want anyone to feel obliged to be here for me.

MICK. But why did she refuse? That's the point. Why? Not because she didn't want to, but because she couldn't face settling down here to a life of false pretences. And yet she felt she couldn't tell you the truth.

GREGORY. The truth? The truth! What truth?

MICK. The truth about herself. (*Turning away to* R. *of grandfather chair.*) I didn't know till last night either. Neither did Jenny. That's all part of the same thing. She could have told us quite easily years ago; but she didn't want to put us in the position of deceiving you all the time. And so she's had to go through the whole thing alone. That's why she's got into this terrible state. The thing has such ramifications . . .

GREGORY. Will you stop ranting and tell me what this is all about?

MICK (*after pause, quietly, stepping forward towards* GREGORY *to* c.). Well, it's perfectly simple. She had an affair with an American airman—it was serious. I mean, she was in love with him. He was killed. In Korea. And after he was killed, she found she was going to have a child.

GREGORY (*after pause*). I see.

MICK (*pause*). Well, don't you see how impossible it would be to tell you a thing like that?

GREGORY. Why impossible?

MICK. Why, isn't it obvious? You're a parson. You'd be shocked. You're bound to be shocked.

GREGORY. Ach, I've no patience with that. D'ye think because I'm a parson I know nothing about life? Why do you suppose I was ever ordained in the first place? D'you think it was because I was so easily shocked that I couldn't face realities?

MICK. No, of course not. That's absurd. But as a parson, you've got a different attitude to life. You think a thing like this that's happened to Margaret is wrong. And what's more you expect other people to look at it that way too. Can't you see? How can parsons expect to be told the truth when one can't even talk to them like ordinary human beings?

GREGORY (*after pause*). If that's the way I've made you all feel . . then I've failed. I've failed completely.

MICK (*pause; looks at him; then, very softly*). Oh, hell . . . (*Goes out through dining-room.*)

(*Pause. MARGARET comes downstairs, dressed for a journey as in Act I, carrying a suitcase. She stops short when she sees her father, feeling trapped. But as he doesn't appear to notice her, she goes on towards hall. Just as she is going out he looks up.*)

GREGORY. Margaret . . . (*She stops in entrance to hall, but does not turn.*) You're going, are you? Ah well, I suppose it's best. Just a moment, though . . . before you go . . . I want you to know that—I know. (*She turns and looks at him steadily.*) Michael's just told me. I can see that you would feel the way you do about it, but . . . I'm sorry, Margaret. It's my fault. I've been no use to you . . . no use at all.

MARGARET (*putting down her suitcase against banister of stairs, and coming to R.C. below grandfather chair, putting on her gloves*). Oh, well, never mind. I managed all right.

GREGORY. That's just what distresses me. I'm not thinking of money or anything like that. But that you felt you *had* to manage alone. And that you've gone on feeling it all these years. That's a terrible thing . . . (*Pause.*) Tell me. Has it always been the same? In the old days, when you were children, did you feel the same way then? Michael tells me you've all of you always been afraid to speak freely before me.

MARGARET. Not for any personal reason. Only because of religion.

GREGORY. Because of religion? (*Pause, then quietly.*) A fine caricature I've made of religion then, if that's how it seems, to me own children . . . It ought to be because of me religion that I'd have more sympathy and understanding for people . . . (*Advancing to below sofa.*) But I have, Margaret, I have. Do I seem the sort of man who'd turn away from the sorrows of his own daughter? (*Going back to fireplace.*) If I do, then no wonder me work's had so little effect all these years. I've been distorting and misrepresenting religion all me life without knowing it . . . I can't believe it . . . Ah well, it's too late now. If that's how it is, you'd better go. You'll be happier in London.

MARGARET. Happy?

GREGORY. At least you've your child.

MARGARET. Didn't Mick tell you? He's dead.

GREGORY (*stepping forward*). Margaret . . .

MARGARET (*stiffens and turns away right*). No, no, please. It's all over and done with now.

GREGORY. But your friends and your work'll be of some help to you?

MARGARET. Friends? (*A step or so towards* C.) My friends are anyone who wants another drink . . . I've often thought how much I'd rather be here. But, of course, it wouldn't work. I know that . . . I'm out all day scribbling smart, highly paid nonsense which earns the rent of a wonderful flat that I can't bear to stay in alone for five minutes when I get back in the evening. It makes no sense. But why should it, after all, if the world as a whole makes no sense?

GREGORY. You mean it makes no sense to you?

MARGARET. No, not only to me. To everyone. Only most people don't notice it. I've been made more aware of it, that's all, because of what's happened.

GREGORY. You mustn't let it make you bitter.

MARGARET. I'm not bitter. This has nothing to do with my personal feelings at all. It's something I've *seen*—just as you suddenly see the solution of a mathematical problem. Only this isn't a solution.

GREGORY. Aren't you deceiving yourself when you say all this has nothing to do with feeling?

MARGARET. I don't think so. (*Breaks* R.) It began with feeling, of course, but feeling soon exhausts itself. You can't feel any emotion, even grief, for ever.

GREGORY. Of course ye can't. But when it's over, you know, Margaret, there's a blankness, there's always a period of . . . of emptiness.

MARGARET. Yes, I know. (*Going to him a little.*) But it's not that. It's something far bigger than that. In that very blankness, I've stumbled on something that affects everyone. Everyone in the world.

> (*The cold force of her tone startles* GREGORY. *Pause, then he turns away to fireplace.*)

(*Quietly, going to* R. *end of sofa.*) Listen. Robert was killed—I really did love him, you know—and after that I found I was going to have Simon. That seemed important. Not only because of Robert, but because, well . . . another life in the world is important. And so, for the next four years, of course, I did everything I possibly could for Simon. Then—he died. And I just felt—what was the point of it all? What was the value of all that effort? Don't you see? (*Sitting on* R. *arm of sofa.*) It was then that I first began to realize that, in the long run, it's the same for everyone. Practically all the efforts that people make are simply to keep life going—their own or someone else's. And the whole thing's doomed to failure. We know that. Life can't be kept going indefinitely. The sun's growing cold and, in the end, the human race itself'll be frozen off the earth. What sense does that make? (*Rising and going up* C.) Oh, I know what you'll say—about immortality and so on. But I just can't believe that. And even if I could, that's not quite the point. I'm not just sentimentally unhappy because I shan't see Bob and Simon again. I'm not the type that starts going to séances because someone I love is dead.

That's not the point. I want to be sure that all the values we try to establish are real values. I want to relate life, here and now, not only my own life, but all life, to whatever may be true about the universe.

GREGORY (*stepping up to* L. *end of sofa*). D'ye know, Margaret, I think you'd be far more comfortable in the world, if you weren't so religious.

MARGARET. I'm not religious. That's the trouble.

GREGORY. But you are, you are. That *is* religion. What you've just been saying.

MARGARET (*moving impatiently over to window*). You don't seem to understand. I don't believe in anything. (*She stands up* C. *of the recess, with her back to him, looking out of the window* L.)

GREGORY. Ach no, it's not belief that's religion. That's not the primary thing at all. There's something else has to be there before that, long before that—something that's the root of all the religions in the world—a need. This feeling ye have—if you stick to it, if you go through with it, if ye're honest about it—this need to make sense of the world; that's the prime essential of all religion.

(*Pause.* MARGARET *stares out of the window. A single bell begins to ring; then another discordantly.* GREGORY *looks at her, hesitates, goes to the stairs. He looks at her again, still staring in silence out of the window.*)

Margaret, I'm sorry. I'd not meant to preach at you.

MARGARET (*turning*). I don't quite know where I am.

GREGORY. Of course you don't.

MARGARET. No, I don't mean that. I mean about you. (*Coming down* C.) You've made it all so difficult.

GREGORY (*annoyed with himself, coming to* R. *of grandfather chair*). Ach, botheration. I'd not meant to say a word. Only while you were speaking just now, it suddenly struck me: these are me own thoughts, this might be meself talking. D'ye know, it was thoughts like yours I had, when I was a young man, that first made me think of being ordained? I'd this need to make sense of the world always tormenting me; and I never could be sure from one day to the next what I believed about anything . . . but do you know what tipped the scales for me? Despair—despair of the kind you've been feeling—despair because there was one fact I didn't see how to make sense of without religion, one fact that knocked the meaning out of any system of morals or politics anyone had ever invented—death. Eat, drink and be merry for to-morrow we die. Perhaps that made sense, I used to think. But struggle for the good of humanity, work for social justice, suffer for an ideal, for to-morrow we die—that didn't seem to make sense at all. Unless . . . unless . . . D'ye see why I felt just now, while you were talkin', these thoughts are my own thoughts? We're very alike, you know, Margaret, you and I. (*Going to hall to get his gum boots.*)

MARGARET (*looking after him*). We are, yes. I see that . . . now. (*Turning away as he comes back.*) That's what I find so bewildering. Our ideas, our beliefs are so different. . . .

GREGORY. Are they?

MARGARET (*turns to face him*). Yes, of course they are. Quite different. But that doesn't make a gulf between us, as I thought it did, because our *minds* are alike. They work the same way . . . *we can talk!* I can't get used to it.

(*Throughout the rest of the scene, she is looking at him a little strangely, as this idea continues to grow on her. She is coming to see him as he really is. It is not her idea of the world which has changed—but her idea of him. GREGORY speaks more or less to himself.*)

GREGORY (*crossing and sitting on sofa to change into his gum boots*). I've always known it. I remember once, when you were quite small—you can't have been more than about six, I suppose—you were sittin' on me knee, looking at a copy of the *Illustrated London News* ; and there was a picture of a judge in his wig. " Oh, look at the funny man in the curls," you said, " what's he? " I told you he was a judge and then you asked me what a judge was. And I was tellin' you. And when I'd finished, there you sat on me knee, starin' at me and frownin'—and d'ye know what you said? " And who judges the judge? " (*He chuckles.*) It's not easy to be comfortable in the world, if you go about askin' awkward, fundamental questions like that. The trouble with you and me is that we can't help askin' them.

MARGARET (*wryly, going to* R. *end of sofa*). And much good it does. Curiosity kills the cat.

GREGORY. They're worth askin', I'm sure of that. Only we mustn't let the questions frighten us . . . nor the possible answers either. I've learned *that* through being a parson anyway. That if ye care for the truth—and ye're no good at all if ye don't, in my opinion—if ye care for the truth and if ye're going to pursue it, even when it means facing answers you don't much fancy, or maybe finding no answers at all, there's something else ye need besides curiosity. To carry you through, you need courage. (*Pause, then suddenly coming out of his reverie.*) Ach, there I go, preachin' again, I suppose. I'm sorry but . . . (*very quietly, staring in front of him.*) I was thinkin' more of meself than of you . . .

MARGARET. Of yourself?

GREGORY. I was talkin' about this very thing to your aunts last night, when they were gettin' at me to retire . . . if you go on year after year in a place like this, makin' no particular impression on anybody, you're bound to wonder sometimes whether ye've drifted out of touch with truth.

MARGARET (*with a shrug*). How can you tell?

GREGORY. Ah, but you can tell sometimes. This talk we've had, Margaret, I know the truth has been in that—if not in the words, then between the words . . . or between us. And that's why I'm grateful to you, for it's not often I have real talk with anyone.

(*The church bells break into a full peal.* GREGORY *jumps up, and takes the last gulp of coffee from his cup on mantelpiece.*)
Ach, good gracious, I'll be late. (*Going towards hall to* R.C. *and putting his shoes down on floor* L. *of him.*)

MARGARET. Your coat? I'll get it. (*She fetches it from hall.*) Here you are. Anything you want from the study?

GREGORY. Me sermon. Ye'll find it lying there on the desk.
(*She goes to fetch it from the study, while he puts on his coat. She returns to* L. *of him.*)
Ach, now what do I do with me shoes? Jenny makes me wear these things for the snow, but I can't take the service in 'em.

MARGARET. Put one in each pocket. (*She does so for him.*) Now, have you got everything you want?

GREGORY. Yes, yes, I think so. Thanks. I'm sorry to rush off like this.

MARGARET. That's all right. (*She kisses him. He begins to go, crossing below her.*) Wait a minute. Your sermon.

GREGORY. Oh . . . ah . . . yes. Thank you. Margaret, I . . . I . . . (*He hesitates at hall opening.*) Oh, well, good-bye. (*He goes, leaving* MARGARET *below grandfather chair.*)

RICHARD (*outside*). Is Margaret there? The car's outside.

GREGORY (*outside*). Yes, yes, she's there! She's all ready.
(*Front door slams.* RICHARD *comes in in overcoat and crosses to fireplace to knock out his pipe.*)

RICHARD. Ready? We ought to go. I couldn't get the car to start.

MARGARET. I'm not going.

RICHARD (*turning*). Oh, my God, women! Do you ever know your own minds? Here have I been working my guts out, trying to get that damn car to start, and you calmly announce that you're not going! What's happened? Had a nice, emotional reconciliation, I suppose. (*Crossing to* L. *of her.*)

MARGARET (*laughing*). How old-fashioned of you, Richard. No. Nothing in the least like that. (*She goes upstairs with her suitcase.*)

RICHARD. Well, I give up. (*He stares after her, puzzled and exasperated.*)
> (*Then he turns swiftly to go out and finds* DAVID *in the doorway.*)

DAVID. Good morning.

RICHARD. Oh, hullo.

DAVID (*hanging his coat up in the hall*). I just walked over to wish you all a Merry Christmas.

RICHARD (*grunts*). Oh.

DAVID. Do you happen to know what Jenny's doing?

RICHARD. Changing her mind, too, I expect. (*He crosses below* DAVID *and goes out, leaving* DAVID *aghast.*)

DAVID. Changing her mind? (*Going to below grandfather chair.*)

> (LYDIA *comes downstairs, dressed for church.*)

LYDIA (*on stairs*). Well, I'll go on then. I must make sure of one of those pews near the radiator. (*Sees* DAVID.) Oh! My poor David. I'm so sorry for you. (*Coming down to* R. *of him.*)

DAVID. Look here, what is all this about?

LYDIA. Well, but . . . oh, hasn't Jenny told you? It's been dreadful, quite dreadful. The most appalling things have happened since you were here yesterday.

DAVID. Yes, but what? That's what I want to know. What's happened?

LYDIA. Oh, dear, I haven't time . . . I'm just going to church . . . (*Going to hall and turning back in the opening.*) But it's all disastrous, absolutely disastrous!

> (BRIDGET *comes downstairs to* R. *of* DAVID.)

BRIDGET (*to* LYDIA). Ach, haven't you gone yet? (*Seeing* DAVID.) Good morning. Ach, there now, I've pulled a hole in me glove.

LYDIA. Oh, by the way, Bridget and I did our best for you and Jenny last night, didn't we Bridget? But I'm afraid it was all no use. (*Goes out through front door.*)

BRIDGET. If you're half a man, you'll get Jenny out of this in double quick time.

DAVID. Out of what? Can *you* tell me what's been happening?

BRIDGET. Ach, it's disgusting. I don't care to talk about it. (*She follows* LYDIA *out.*)

(MICK *hurries through from dining-room into hall for his coat.*)

MICK. Oh, hullo David. (*Getting his coat.*) Everything's hell here this morning. I got tight last night. (*Returning with his coat to* R. *of* DAVID, *and putting it on.*)

DAVID. Is that all? They've been making such a song and dance about it, I thought it was serious. (*Sitting on arm of grandfather chair.*)

MICK. Serious! It's serious enough in this house. It's shaken the whole foundations. I'm going to be late for church.

DAVID. Church? You?

MICK. Well, you feel you have to more or less. I mean, it's a matter of politeness, really, when your old man's a parson. Especially on Christmas Day. Margaret got tight too, last night. She passed out. She's leaving for London by the next train.

DAVID (*rising and turning* MICK *to face him*). What? But she *can't* . . . besides she only arrived last night.

MICK. Since last night there's been an atomic explosion. The whole of our lives have been split open, exposed. This morning everyone's stumbling about among the debris. The whole place is radio-active. I must go. Oh! Wait a minute. Can you lend me sixpence?

DAVID. What for?

MICK. The collection.

DAVID. Oh, aye. (*Gives it to him.*)

MICK. Jenny will pay you back out of the housekeeping—I hope. (*He goes out.*)

(MARGARET *comes downstairs and stops on first step.*)

MARGARET (*seeing* DAVID). Good morning.

DAVID (*going to her*). You'll be Margaret, I suppose. Look here, I've a bone to pick with you. What's all this about you refusing to come home? I've no patience with it. You've got to take your turn.

MARGARET (*quietly, smiling at him*). But I am coming home.

DAVID. You are! There now. I said you would.

MARGARET. Did you?

DAVID. I told Jenny yesterday. I couldn't believe it when she said you wouldn't.

MARGARET. I wonder why she thought I wouldn't . . .

DAVID. I don't know. She said you just wouldn't. You weren't that sort of a person. I thought it was monstrous.

MARGARET. You remind me of my Aunt Bridget. You seem to have very explosive views about people.

DAVID. I just see them clearly, that's all.

MARGARET. Black and white. The cartoon mind. (*She moves below him and towards dining-room to up* C. *to look for* JENNY.) Be careful you don't see them too clearly.

DAVID. I don't see there's any danger in that.

MARGARET (*turning to him*). I'm not sure it's not one of the greatest dangers in the world. You can see people perfectly clearly and yet know nothing of what they really are. I thought I knew someone. (*Coming down to* R. *end of sofa.*) I thought I knew him so well that I could tell exactly what he'd say or do in any situation, down to the smallest inflection of his voice. And now I find I've never really known him at all. It's *frightening* how little, really, one knows about other people.

DAVID (*going to* L. *of her*). I don't know that it particularly frightens me.

MARGARET. It should, I think. Certainly if you're going to marry.

DAVID. Look here, what are you getting at? I can't make head or tail of anyone in this house this morning. What's the matter with you all?

MARGARET. Christmas. The family festival. We've all learnt a thing or two about each other, that's all.

(*The peal changes to the single note of the five-minute bell.*)

I must go. I'll be late for church. (*Crossing below him to hall and turning in opening.*) Look, I haven't had time to see Jenny. You must tell her. Perhaps it'll be better for you to tell her, anyway. Tell her—that I've had some talk with my father, and that *it's all quite all right*, that last bit's the most important. She'll know what it means.

DAVID. Don't worry. She'll know what it means all right.

MARGARET (*in hall opening*). I wonder how well you know Jenny . . . I wonder if you know in the least what she's really like?

DAVID. I've a pretty shrewd idea.

MARGARET. After this morning I'm inclined to think it takes more than shrewdness to understand *any* human being. Good luck. (*She goes out by front door.*)

DAVID (*stands looking after her, then follows her to opening to call after her*). A happy Christmas to you!

MARGARET (*outside, gaily*). Thank you.

(*The five-minute bell is still ringing. Enter JENNY from dining-room.*)

JENNY. David . . .

DAVID (*turns and sees her*). Jenny!

JENNY. Oh, David! Wait a moment. I must just see if Daddy's gone. (*Coming to up C.*)

DAVID (*going up to L. of her*). Jenny, *Margaret's coming home.*

JENNY. Oh, but she mustn't.

DAVID. Mustn't! D'ye mean—you've changed your mind?

JENNY. No, but . . .

DAVID. Well what does *this* mean then? She's just this minute told me to tell you she's had some talk with your father and it's quite all right. (JENNY *just stares.*) Well?

JENNY. Oh, that's wonderful. It won't be easy, of course . . . but it's . . . everything! (*She burst into tears of relief.*)

DAVID. Jenny . . . Jenny . . . what's the matter? . . . What are ye crying for? . . . (*Then explosively.*) I think ye're mad!

CURTAIN.

THE END OF THE PLAY.

PROPERTY PLOT

ACT I

Centre: step-ladder under chandelier, steps upstage. Downstage of it—dust sheet on floor, with holly and ivy.

Fireplace: small pile of logs. In cupboard upstage of it—bottle of whisky, nearly full. On cupboard—wireless set.

Sofa table: cigarette box, ashtray, matches.

Hall stand: Gregory's coat, scarf and gloves, torch in drawer.

Chair down R.C. (back to audience)—box of decorations with star, coloured string, 2 pieces of ivy.

Offstage: dining-room — tray with water jug and 2 glasses; front door— 3 suitcases (Lydia), 1 suitcase (Bridget), 1 suitcase (Richard), 1 suitcase (Margaret).

ACT II

STRIKE dust sheet with holly and ivy from grandfather chair; box of decorations from sofa table; logs from fire.

Cupboard above fire: Harper's Magazine, book.

Sofa table: tray with coffee for 7, cigarette box with two cigarettes, ashtray and matches.

Hall stand: Margaret's coat and scarf, Mick's overcoat.

Mantelpiece: shilling.

Sofa: Margaret's handbag, magazine.

Table at double doors—tray with whisky, water jug and 2 glasses, ashtray.

Offstage: dining-room—tray with tea for 6, kettle; study—cigar box, book; stairs R.—2 workbags.

NOTE: Curtains closed at windows and hall. Holly set by David and Mick re-arranged.

ACT III

STRIKE tea-tray, whisky tray, workbags, Margaret's bag and scarf.

Table in recess: 7 piles of Christmas presents, 1 containing Eau de Cologne.

Honesty.

Mantelpiece: Christmas card with kitten.

Table at double doors: ashtray.

Hall stand: Gregory's coat, scarf and gum boots, Richard's coat and cap, Mick's coat.

Offstage: dining-room—table napkin, cup of coffee, tray with coffee and 1 cup, apron; study—sermon; stairs —presents for Bridget, 1 containing bed cape, presents for Richard, Margaret's suitcase.

NOTE: All curtains open, snow covered tree outside window.

Lightning Source UK Ltd.
Milton Keynes UK
UKHW022000220522
403359UK00005B/105

9 780573 111938